PARENTS, CHILDREN
AND
THE FACTS OF LIFE

PARENTS, CHILDREN
AND
THE FACTS OF LIFE

A TEXT ON SEX EDUCATION FOR
CHRISTIAN PARENTS AND FOR THOSE
CONCERNED WITH HELPING PARENTS

By

Fr. Henry V. Sattler, C.SS.R., Ph.D.

Assistant Director, Family Life Bureau,
National Catholic Welfare Conference

With a Foreword by

Francis J. Connell, C.SS.R., S.T.D.

Professor Emeritus of Moral Theology,
Catholic University of America

TAN Books
Charlotte, North Carolina

IMPRIMI POTEST: John Sephton, C.SS.R.
                   Provincial Superior
                   October 13, 1951

NIHIL OBSTAT: Bede Babo, O.S.B.
                   Censor Librorum

IMPRIMATUR: ✛ Thomas A. Boland
                   Bishop of Paterson
                   October 22, 1952

Originally published by St. Anthony Guild Press, Paterson, N.J., in January 1953 and reprinted September 1953, February 1955 and again in 1961. Also published by Doubleday in the Image Book series in 1956 and reprinted by them numerous times. (Total copies printed prior to the TAN edition: approx. 750,000.)

Reprinted with permission of The Franciscans, St. Anthony's Guild, Paterson, New Jersey 07509-2948.

Library of Congress Catalog Card No.: 93-60170

ISBN 978-0-89555-489-5

Printed and bound in the United States of America.

TAN Books
Charlotte, North Carolina
1993

To
Saint Maria Goretti
Martyred for Her Love of
Chastity and Modesty

ACCLAMATIONS OF THIS BOOK . . .

". . . because of widespread appeal from parents asking for such a work I am happy to voice approval of this popular book by Father Sattler, *Parents, Children and the Facts of Life.*"
—Most Rev. Edwin V. O'Hara, Archbishop
Chairman, Episcopal Committee
Confraternity of Christian Doctrine

"This work is by far the best on the subject produced to date. . . clear, forceful, definitive. . .the last word in Christian Sex Education."
—Dr. Alphonse Clemens, Director
Marriage Counseling Center Catholic University

"This is, perhaps, the best, the most complete, and the most practical treatment of the whole question of sex education yet written by a Catholic."
—*Catholic Transcript*

"For practicality, precision of detail, thoroughness of treatment combined with compactness of volume, we do not know the equal of this book in the sex education field."
—*The Register*

"A providential answer to a problem which we who are concerned with education find more pressing month by month. . . I thank God for its existence."
—Msgr. Sylvester J. Holbel
Superintendent of Catholic Schools, Buffalo

"Seldom has a manual been written which fills so adequately the purpose for which it is intended."
—*The Magnificat*

vii

Publisher's Preface

Parents, Children and the Facts of Life is undoubtedly the most successful Catholic book ever written on the duties of parents to instruct their children properly concerning sex and procreation. Among the four printings of the book published by St. Anthony Guild Press, starting in 1953, and the numerous printings done in the Doubleday Image edition, some 750,000 copies of this book have been sold, according to the author's own reckoning.

Originally writing between 1947 and 1949, the author labored over every line to be certain that every word he wrote was in strict accord with the teaching of the Catholic Church regarding parental duties concerning educating children in the facts of life. Fr. Francis J. Connell, C.SS.R., S.T.D., then Dean of the School of Sacred Theology at Catholic University of America, had been asked by the U.S. National Catholic Welfare Conference to write this book, but because he was too busy, he in turn commissioned Fr. Sattler to do it; nonetheless, Fr. Connell "guided it every step of the way," to use Fr. Sattler's own words.

The result is a book which is eminently helpful to parents, that they may know, not only their duties in this delicate and important matter, but also what techniques and methods to employ. A thorough reading of *Parents, Children and the Facts of Life* will give all parents the necessary tools to handle this important aspect of their role as the primary educators of their children.

One might think that the passage of forty years from

the printing of the first edition of the book would have rendered it outmoded or grossly dated. But exactly the opposite is the case. Except for the dates in the footnotes and bibliography, the text reads as fresh as if it had been written today. Virtually every reference, for example, to the baneful influence of the secular world on the tender consciences of children today is as accurate and meaningful now as it was when written— except that today serious Catholic parents realize even more profoundly what a stark contrast exists between the "sex education" imparted in the public schools and by way of the media and entertainment business, on the one hand, and what should be imparted in a proper Catholic context and manner, on the other. In a letter of February 1, 1993 to the present Publisher, the author confessed, "I have often attempted to revise and update and re-edit the book, but it would never lend itself to revision, as though cast in iron which would not 'mill.'" What the author has produced in this book is a classic, timeless, Catholic statement on the role of parents *vis-à-vis* the education of their children in the facts of life. It does not need to be changed.

As the reader gets into the book, it may appear overly long and needlessly protracted, but the fact is that parents should keep reading, right to the end, and make the contents of this book their own, so that when an occasion arises to make a point in the sexual education of one of their children, the instruction can be done immediately, simply, naturally, and just to the extent needed by that child at that time. For the intent of this book is to *form* the parent to become a confident, effective, proper teacher in this subject for his or her own children. If a parent will read the book through and digest its contents, it will produce the desired effect.

Finally, Fr. Henry V. Sattler's *Parents, Children and the Facts of Life* will serve as an excellent and much-needed counterpoise to the Godless, public and grossly immodest "sex education" employed in the public schools—and, alas, in all too many Catholic schools.

For it will give parents at once both the ammunition to show school authorities that the primary and essential obligation to instruct their own children in sexual matters belongs to THE PARENT and not the school, plus it will more than equip parents for their task.

It is a pleasure, then, to present to the reader this extremely important and germane little book.

The Publisher
February 9, 1993

FOREWORD

The right and duty to educate children belongs in the first place to those who gave them life, their parents. Indeed, the education of the young is so intimately bound up with parenthood that the Catholic Church has always regarded it as pertaining to the primary end of matrimony. Parents may—and usually do—depute to professional teachers the task of instructing their boys and girls in the various branches of natural knowledge that make up the curriculum of schools and colleges. Catholic parents may delegate even a portion of the spiritual training of their children to the teachers in the parochial schools. But parents may not entirely consign to others the task of providing for the moral and religious formation of their sons and daughters. Almighty God, who has conferred on a married couple the privilege of bringing children into the world, has commanded that they actively and earnestly help those children to know, love and serve Him in this life, so that they will be happy with Him forever in the life beyond the grave.

One of the most important phases in this parental duty of promoting the spiritual welfare of the young is sex education. Unfortunately, to many parents this means nothing more than the imparting of biological facts concerning the process of procreation and the measures to be taken in order to avoid disease. To Catholics, sex education means much more than this. It signifies, primarily, the training of boys and girls to be pure and innocent, and eventually to enter marriage with a noble and holy purpose, if God calls them to that state of life.

However, as most parents would readily admit, the proper fulfillment of this task is by no means easy. The embarrassment that is likely to accompany the frank discussion of so delicate and personal a matter, the difficulty of choosing the right terms, and the fear that the child will ask questions which they may not be able to answer deter many parents from undertaking their duty, despite the unquestionable fact that in this age of blatant indecency and sexual license the proper sex education of adolescents is vitally necessary if their chastity is to be preserved.

The present volume is intended to help parents fulfill this particular duty in the training of their boys and girls. Father Sattler has treated the subject clearly and thoroughly. What parents should tell their children, when and how they should tell it, what psychological and moral dangers they must avoid in giving sex instruction, what questions they must expect—these and many other pertinent problems are discussed in detail and answered in a simple and sensible manner.

In propounding the method to be followed and the expressions to be employed for imparting sex information, Father Sattler has avoided two extremes which could easily spoil the instruction: on the one hand, vague and unsatisfying statements which are likely to arouse undue curiosity, and on the other hand, vivid and stimulating descriptions that may be a proximate occasion of sin to youthful hearers. Parents who follow the plan suggested in this book will do more than give their children all the knowledge they need at the appropriate time. They will also impart it in a calm and natural way that causes no emotional shock but rather instills into the minds of their boys and girls a spirit of respect and reverence for the sexual power whereby human beings can co-operate with God toward the propagation of citizens for the Kingdom of Heaven.

Father Sattler bases his teachings on the rules laid down by the Catholic Church for the sex training of the young, and particularly on the directions given by two of our recent Popes, Pius XI and Pius XII. He emphasizes the important fact that innocence (which is most desirable) is very different from ignorance (which may be a grave menace to the innocence of adolescents in this godless age). And he consistently applies the accepted principles of Catholic theology to the many concrete cases which constitute a very practical feature of this book.

In the questions and discussion aids which are found at the end of each chapter Father Sattler has made a distinctively valuable pedagogical contribution. Parents who give serious thought to these problems will find their understanding of the text clarified and co-ordinated. The benefit is greatly increased when a group of parents discuss these points frankly and honestly. It should likewise be noted that this book will also help teachers to discover and fulfill their function in chastity education as delegates and helpers in what is essentially a parental duty.

Although much that is contained in this book could be utilized with profit by persons of any religious creed, the book is intended primarily for Catholic parents. The Catholic Church is fully aware that the faith and loyalty of her members can be best assured when they possess an intelligent and logical grasp of the Church's teachings. For this reason, the Confraternity of Christian Doctrine approves this work as an outstanding contribution toward promoting a better understanding of Catholic teaching and toward inspiring both parents and children to practice fervently the glorious virtue of chastity, to which the Son of God attached the sublime promise: "Blessed are the clean of heart, for they shall see God."

FRANCIS J. CONNELL, C. SS. R., S. T. D.
Professor Emeritus of Moral Theology
Catholic University of America

INTRODUCTION

Did a faint glimmer of hope spring up in your mind as you took this book down from the shelf or out of its wrapper? Did you say, perhaps: "At last, a book on sex education for ordinary parents, and not for teachers or for the children themselves"? Or were you rather skeptical: "Another book on sex education? I wonder whether this one will really help?" Yes, Dad or Mother, this book is really for you. It is not directed *at* you like a command or a sermon, but it's an answer to your own demand. The Parent-Educator Committee of the Confraternity of Christian Doctrine, under a barrage of appeals from parents, asked the author to attempt this work. Not only is this book written *for* you and at your demand, but, to a large extent, it was written *by* you, since nearly every practical hint in its pages has come from parents themselves. The author has merely supplied the scientific framework, and the emotional, moral and religious setting within which your practical ideas have been or can be utilized.

Have you hesitated to educate your children in matters of sex? If so, has your indecision arisen from the constant disputes of the specialists? (For example, "Bathe young children of both sexes together." "No, don't do that!"—"Tell them all the facts at once, and early." "It is best to tell them the facts gradually."—"Give them a birds-and-bees story." "You'll only confuse them if you do!"—"Always use medical terms." "Don't use medical terms.") We are hopeful that this book will enable you to judge the value of such statements and choose the safe and correct procedure in your home.

Have you shrunk from your duty because it seemed to demand specialized training? Too long have you been the whipping posts of the specialists. Logically, they are likely to say that you no longer have the right to bear children. By scathing criticism and technical language, the specialists have persuaded many a parent to give the child's body entirely to doctors, his mind to teachers, his emotions and character to psychiatrists. Such a parent will not make a move without consulting a trained person. This is foolish because common sense is still one of the best ways to approach reality. Specialists certainly have their value in *helping you* to bring up your children. You learn about hygiene from a doctor, or you call him in when you meet an insurmountable problem like a broken leg. But when your child skins his knee, you yourself are a "general practitioner" of medicine. In the same way, with the help of this book you can make yourself a general practitioner of sex education. You need a specialist only for insoluble cases.

Have your own experiences in this matter of sex education puzzled you? Do you think you received too little, or too much, sex education? Do you feel that the pagan surroundings in which your child must live demand special helps which you are not qualified to give? This volume will help you form some definite answers to these questions.

Lastly, do you fear that your sex instruction might endanger your children's chastity instead of protecting it? We hope that these pages will give you a confidence which, tempered with caution, will fit you to judge what to say and what to do.

To make the best use of the ideas within these covers, we suggest that you discuss them with others. We have in mind Parent-Educator Discussion Clubs, Cana Clubs, Parent-Teacher Associations, and similar groups, especially if both men and women are included in them. If you do not belong to such a group, or cannot form one, at least try to discuss the material with your husband or wife.

Discussion is valuable for many reasons. *First,* it will make you familiar with the correct words. If you can clearly and chastely express yourself on sex to some adult, you will find it easier to express yourself to your children. *Second,* such discussions will create an attitude of calmness and a sensible confidence in your own common sense and abilities. *Third,* discussion will help make difficult points clear. If two or more people thrash out the meaning of a paragraph, they can more easily avoid misunderstanding it. *Fourth,* the sexes think and feel differently. Indeed, the experience of maturing sexually is to some extent different for every man and woman. If all pool their information, they will understand their boys and girls better and will more neatly adapt their helps to the needs of each age and sex. *Fifth,* parents on the same footing in society will find common problems arising, for example, problems concerning dating, dress, curfew, etc. Common action will be more effective in bringing about sensible reforms. *And last,* discussion in groups will convince you that, despite many individual differences, the experiences of parents are remarkably similar. Such a conviction will relieve you of a number of needless worries.

The questions added at the end of each chapter will facilitate discussion. But beware! The questions are not of the usual sort. They will not only ask you what you have learned from the chapter, but they will also propose problems for solution. Sometimes solutions will be suggested and sometimes not. The wish is to stimulate your Catholic observation, judgment, and reasonable action. Should these questions seem too numerous, check those you think most important before you discuss a chapter. If several people of your group check the same five or six questions, they are the important questions for you.

The length and detail of this book might tempt you to throw up your hands in despair because there seems to be so much to remember. But in fact there is very little. The book is long because there are so many false ideas on sex education to be refuted. Once this has been done, and you have absorbed the right sane and healthy attitudes, you need memorize only a few facts, a few terms, and a few moral principles—four, to be exact. Surely, any grade school graduate is capable of understanding and using the ideas in these pages.

Though written for parents, and indeed, *because* written for parents, this volume should also be of value for teachers and priests. The material contained here will enable them to support and help parents in their duty of sex education. The various chapters will also aid teachers and priests to find their own place when and if it becomes necessary to supplement parental work, or perhaps to supply parental omissions. BUT, ABOVE ALL, THIS BOOK SHOULD HELP PREVENT THE DISAS-TROUS ERROR OF TAKING ONE MORE PARENTAL FUNCTION OUT OF THE HOME.

That your mind may be at rest concerning the reliability of this work, it should be mentioned that it has been subjected to a double ecclesiastical censorship, and has received the approval, besides, of a wide variety of experts: two Catholic teachers in public schools, three lay-religious teachers in Catholic high schools, three nuns, all experienced teachers, two doctors, two moral theologians, two psychiatrists, a psychiatrist-philosopher, a pastor of some twenty-five years' experience, a successful counselor of adolescents, three experienced parish missionaries, a sociologist of some renown in the field of marriage, and some ten married couples with children of various ages. It also has the full approbation of the national Confraternity of Christian Doctrine.

HENRY V. SATTLER, C. SS. R., Ph. D.
FAMILY LIFE BUREAU, N. C. W. C.

CONTENTS

PARENTS, CHILDREN
AND
THE FACTS OF LIFE

Chapter I
Getting Our Bearings

There is scarcely a field in which the terms are so unsettled as in the field of sex education. For one thing, these terms have many shades of meaning, which often vary with the person using them. Again, some of the words are long and cumbersome; yet in many cases we must use these technical words if we are not to use the vulgar words.

The best thing, then, is to begin at the beginning by learning the expressions and the meanings we shall need.

SEX

This is a "scare word" in much of modern speech and writing. To most people it means the *bodily* differences between male and female and the intense pleasure associated with the organs of sex. This latter is called sex pleasure, or venereal pleasure. It is unfortunate that the word "sex" has become associated so exclusively with the act of sexual union. (Sexual union is the act by which children are begotten; also called the *marital act, marital intercourse, coitus,* or *sexual relations.*) Actually, an individual is a member of his sex in every fiber of his being, not only in those physical organs by which he differs from the other sex. A man is a man, and a woman is a woman, in thinking, reasoning, feeling, emotions, and in bodily characteristics. *The true meaning of sex is this: the God-given charac-*

ter of being male or female. The physical differences
are an indication of a complete difference between the
sexes in every sphere, for the sexes could not be more
different than they are and remain members of the
human race.

The word "intercourse" has come to signify the act
of sexual union. When coupled with the word "marital" or "conjugal," scarcely any other meaning is accepted
by the modern mind. It should mean mutual exchange,
communication, fellowship. Even marital intercourse
should mean the whole common life, the give-and-take
of husband and wife in married life, and not merely
their physical relations.

SEX EDUCATION—SEX INSTRUCTION

If, taken strictly, "sex" means the character of being
male or female, then "sex education" should mean the
education of a boy to be a man and of a girl to be a
woman. "Sex instruction" should mean the imparting
of those facts which a man or woman should know. As
a matter of fact, in popular usage, these phrases do
not mean that. Even "education" and "instruction" are
not definite terms. Many people use one for the other,
but strictly speaking, *instruction* means imparting
knowledge. A boy is instructed in history or mathematics. *Education* means the systematic cultivation of all
the natural powers of a person. It means not only information, but training. A child is educated when he has
all the information, attitudes, religious and moral training, and emotional growth that he should have at his
level of development. Instruction may stop at any age.
Education can and should continue for life.

To get down to our topic—what is sex education? As
stated above, the term should mean the developing of
a boy to full manhood and of a girl to full womanhood.
It is too bad that we cannot use the term in that sense,
but if we did, we would not be understood. For our purpose, then, sex education will mean the full training

of boys and girls to enable them to meet and solve the problems that arise in connection with the instinct of procreation. It includes the necessary instruction in the "facts of life," but it goes far beyond that. Good sex education includes training in attitudes toward this problem, the teaching of religious and moral principles, safeguarding the emotional approaches, as well as many other, lesser things; all of which will provide a mature outlook on the so-called sexual problem.

A boy or girl who knows all the "facts of life" is instructed in sex, but is he or she educated? Does the boy or girl know when the sexual functions are to be exercised? Do they know what is right or wrong concerning sex? Have they learned self-control? How does the growing girl feel about motherhood? Does the boy look upon the girl merely as a source of physical pleasure, or as a future mother, companion and helpmate? The correct answers to these and a hundred other questions will indicate whether one is *educated* in this matter. Mere instruction on the "facts of life" may take but a few minutes. Sex education takes the whole lifetime of the child from its earliest years up to maturity.

CHASTITY

Ultimately, sex education means training in the virtues which regulate the sexual appetite. These virtues are chastity and modesty. What is chastity? "It is," says Davis, "the moral virtue that controls in the married, and altogether excludes in the unmarried, all voluntary expression of the appetite for venereal pleasure."[1] *All voluntary expression,* let us repeat, whether in thought, desire or act.

Chastity is to be practiced by every human being. Married people sometimes think that, since only religious take a "vow of chastity," the married cannot possess this virtue. On the contrary, there is a law of

---

1. Davis, Henry, S. J., *Moral and Pastoral Theology* (Sheed and Ward, New York), II, p. 172. Here and elsewhere this work is quoted with permission of the publisher.

chastity for married people, regulating their use of vene-real pleasure, and therefore a virtue of chastity that they must practice. Priests and religious bind themselves to practice virginal chastity, that is, to avoid *all* voluntary venereal pleasure in thought, desire and action. Husbands and wives must practice the chastity of their state; that is, they must avoid all acts, desires and thoughts contrary to the rights of marriage. For an individual to remain chaste throughout life means that he abstains from all willful sexual activity while he remains unmarried; and that in marriage he uses his sexual functions without sin.

It is common to speak of purity as identical with chastity; and though, strictly speaking, we may use the term "purity" in reference to other than sexual matters, we shall accept the identity here. The vice opposed to chastity, or purity, is called unchastity or, more commonly, impurity.

MODESTY

Many people confuse purity or chastity with modesty. There is a relation between them, but one is not the other. Modesty is the hedge which surrounds and protects chastity. "Modesty is the virtue which controls those acts which, though not evil in themselves, may induce in oneself or in others an incitement to lust or venereal pleasure" (*ibid.*). For example, an impure thought would be the voluntary imagination of oneself enjoying illicit venereal pleasure. An immodest thought *might* be the image of the nude form of a person of the other sex. A scanty bathing suit would be *immodest* dress; it could not rightly be called *impure*. A caress could be an immodest action because it might cause impure feelings. Fornication (sexual intercourse between unmarried persons) or masturbation (indulging in complete sexual pleasure alone) are impure, or unchaste, acts.

Both chastity and modesty come under the Sixth and Ninth Commandments. *Deliberate unchaste acts are always mortal sins.* Immodest acts may be *mortal, venial,* or *no sin at all.*[2]

These distinctions will be fully clarified in our treatment of the moral principles concerning sex (Chapters VII and VIII).

INNOCENCE—IGNORANCE

A young child is both ignorant and innocent of many things. He is ignorant of these things because he lacks knowledge of them. He is innocent because he is free from the taint of evil or personal sin. In its strictest sense, innocence means freedom from the personal experience of evil or sin. Now, a child may be ignorant of many things in the sexual sphere and yet be far from innocent. He may not know all the purposes of his body, yet he may have contracted an evil habit which he knows is sinful; for example, masturbation. On the other hand, he may be far from ignorant and yet innocent. He may know the essential "facts of life" and still remain pure.

Though *ignorance* of many facts may help in early life to safeguard a child's innocence, after a certain time ignorance is, if anything, a danger to his innocence. For example, if at the end of grade school a boy were still ignorant of the holy purpose of his sexual organs, his innocence would certainly be endangered. Such a boy might be led into evil habits without realizing it until they became almost too strong to be overcome. Therefore a child should not be kept ignorant of a reasonable amount of sex knowledge in accordance with his age. This knowledge is good and concerns a good thing, because sexual things are good; indeed, they are holy, since they are created by God.

On the other hand, it may be said in general that a child should be *ignorant of evil* as long as is reason-

---

2. Taken strictly, only an act which is judged to be sinful is immodest. An act which is usually immodest, but which might be justified in certain circumstances, is not in those circumstances against modesty.

ably possible. We mean by this that he should not have even a theoretical knowledge of sexual sins until such knowledge is needful for him. St. Thomas warns us that too much consideration of vile things distracts us from good thoughts, and because of our fallen human nature, thoughts of evil may captivate our wills.[3] Despite this danger, however, some theoretical knowledge of evil is progressively necessary exactly in order that a growing youth, by building up his defenses against evil, may maintain his innocence.

This discussion about innocence and two kinds of ignorance can best be illustrated from the story of the Annunciation (*Luke* 1:26-38). Our Blessed Lady was certainly innocent of all sin. Probably, she was also *ignorant* of sexual crimes and abuses. Nevertheless, her understanding of the angel's message, and her question—"How shall this happen, since I do not know man?"—show that she knew the ordinary sexual facts of procreation, conception and birth. According to tradition, at the time of the Annunciation Our Lady was between fourteen and sixteen years of age.

KNOWING WORDS AND IGNORANCE

We must not confuse knowledge of certain sexual words with genuine knowledge. Many children can use very "knowing" terms which nevertheless cloak a startling ignorance. Sometimes a child will speak knowingly, but only in order to learn more without asking a direct question. Parents must learn to judge what is behind such words. They are the only ones who can. Adolescents are anxious never to admit to their companions that they are in the dark on the subject of sex. Some even pretend to a lack of innocence; it is considered "smart" to lay claim to great sins in this regard. This makes it very difficult for the inquiring adolescent to know what is right and good. Therefore, par-

---

3. Cf. *Summa Theologica*, II-II, q. 81, a. 8; q. 82. a. 3, ad 1.

ents must be extremely watchful and intelligent in guiding them.

Sex Education As Part of General Education

The modern world has an odd approach to life. So many people live their lives in compartments. They speak of religious life, home life, business life, and even sex life, as if these various spheres were boxed-off areas of activity without relationship to one another. To many, religion has come to mean going to church on Sunday, and nothing more. How often have you heard it said that religion has no place in politics, no place in business? Again, medicine has been largely divorced from morality. Law has become impersonal and often takes little account of human factors. Sex has become a department of life, a series of personal experiments cut off from everything else, at times not even connected with marriage. Very few people have really tried to integrate their living into a unified pattern.

Many an educator has accepted this error. He is like a chemist before his row of bottles. He uses, let us say, two drops of mathematics, three of history, three of geography, two of English, one drop of religion, and three drops of sex instruction. No wonder the mixture at times becomes explosive! There is no plan or order in such education; no unity, in which every part of life has its proper relation to every other part.

This holds above all for sex education. Sex is not a special subject to be taught at a special place or at a special time. It is true that in this book we are making a study of this one side of life. But that is for the instruction of parents and teachers. We must warn against the temptation to try to teach "sex" as a particular "branch of knowledge" to a child. Such an effort could well be disastrous. It cannot be repeated too often that mature education on sexual matters is only one fiber in the fabric of life.

If sex education is made an isolated process, we shall

never succeed in educating the child to a chaste life. The reason is simple. There is scarcely a stronger impulse in human beings than the sexual impulse. Our fallen nature, under the curse of original sin, tends downward; and children, besides, have the weakness of childhood. If sex is singled out for separate study by a child, his attention is focused, without any sort of protective balance, upon his most passionate impulses. The result can only be unwholesome curiosity, dangerous imaginings, passionate stirrings, and ultimately, complete loss of self-control. Therefore, though we are concentrating on the principles of sex education in this book, IN THE ACTUAL INSTRUCTION OF CHILDREN THESE PRINCIPLES MUST NOT BE SEPARATED FROM THE PRINCIPLES COVERING THEIR TRAINING IN GENERAL.

THE PURPOSE OF SEX EDUCATION

The purpose of Christian sex education is to train to chaste living. This involves two important aims which Christian parents must constantly keep in mind:

1. Children must be taught how to be absolutely virginal until marriage, or for life if their vocation is to the celibate state.[4]

2. Children must be educated in such a way that they may properly and chastely exercise their powers of procreation if and when they marry.

These two aims of sex education are not contradictory; in fact, they are the two halves of the only proper kind of sex education. The best preparation for a chaste marriage is a chaste unmarried life. Yet any teaching that makes the child unfit for either state is wrong. If a prudish or shamefaced or what may be called a "dirty" approach is used on (or permitted to be adopted by)

---

4. Celibacy is the state of being unmarried. Virginity is the intentional achievement of abstaining from voluntary venereal pleasure. This achievement may be for a time, for example, until marriage, or for life, in which case it is called perfect virginity. Cf. Aertnys, J.-Damen, C. A., *Theologia Moralis* (Marietti, Turin, 1950), I, # # 594-595.

the child, then marriage will be degraded and the child will not grow up to become a fit husband or wife, father or mother. If an open, brash, "I-tell-my-child-everything" attitude is adopted, then the child may be endangered in his premarital or lifetime purity.

AVOIDING EXTREMES

As you read this book, you will again and again meet problems which might be approached from either of two completely opposite attitudes. A common-sense, middle course will invariably be the proper approach. The teaching of the Catholic Church never satisfies the extremists. In her doctrines on property and labor, she is attacked by both Communists and extreme capitalists. In matters of sex and chastity she does not satisfy the fleshly who want all knowledge to be imparted from the beginning, because she is mindful of the spirit and of man's fallen nature. She does not satisfy the puritans who believe in ignoring the subject, because she knows that the body is good and holy. She remembers that man is not all soul nor all body; that the two elements are essentially united to make up his being.

A sensible middle course is necessary for instructions on modesty of dress and of the eyes, for the proper attitude toward romantic love, for training the emotions, and for a hundred other things. In your own doubts, always try to steer a middle course. If you are in this middle path between extremes, you are usually in the right.

REALISM

Today realism is often taken to mean emphasis on the brutal, harsh, disgusting things of life. The term "realistic" is applied to a novel if it describes vulgar (and usually sexual) affairs. This is false realism. On the other hand, there is a false romanticism or idealism that refuses to face certain realities at all. In sex education, both false realism and false romanticism are to be condemned. The only sane approach is to be found in true and forthright realism, which faces the fact that there are both good and evil in life and that every human being should recognize them both and be able to do something about them.

> Realism does not consist in ignoring the pageant of suffering. . . . Nor does it consist in merely noting it with however artistic or journalistic an eye for the grimmest and most revolting details. Realism consists in accepting personal responsibility as the only realistic way of setting out to do something about it.[5]

Thus we must see and judge life as it is—a mixture of the bright and the dark, of the happy and the sad, of the laborious and the pleasurable, full of temptations to be faced and of victories to be won.

In sex matters, it is not realistic to ignore the facts of temptation, sin, or even perversion, nor to gloss them over as if there were no such things. Nor is it realistic to make the bad seem good or the good bad. It is realistic only to recognize both evil and good and to realize one's responsibilities.

You who are parents must be realistic with your children. Your child is capable of both evil and good. He has the same sexual temptations, the same problems, the same chances for victory, that you had and that all children have. He or she can sin! Teach your children to be realistic. Teach them that there is both pain and pleasure in life; that life is a struggle, but a worthwhile struggle; that sex presents problems that must be met and solved; that marriage is an adventure, a test, a challenge to manhood and womanhood. In other words, your children must be taught to face both good and bad in life without allowing either to absorb all their attention. One who has eyes for only the good or

---

5. Luce, Clare Boothe, "The Real Reason," in *McCall's Magazine*, February, 1947, p. 117. Quoted with permission of the publisher.

the bad, for only the romance or only the trials, is unprepared for life as it is. Neurotics are those who cannot face the real order of things, which includes both the pleasant and the unpleasant. We do not mean that the child's natural romanticism should be stifled; but the child should be made aware of the difficulties it will have to face in life.

QUESTIONS AND DISCUSSION AIDS

1. Does the word "sex" refer only to the organs which distinguish the male and female body? What is sex in its wide, general meaning? Use these words correctly in sentences expressing some phase of sexual information: procreation, venereal, relations, intercourse, marital, male, female, coitus. How many of these words can you use in sentences not applying to venereal acts? (You should be able to use all but three; in doubt, consult a dictionary.)

2. What is the difference between instruction and education? In your youth, were you well educated in chastity? Could you have been instructed without being educated, or educated without being instructed?

3. Will the meaning of "sex" and "education" make any difference when you discuss the problem of "sex education in the schools" with non-Catholics? Suppose that, to them, sex education means teaching physiology and facts about venereal disease? Suppose it means what you mean, would it make any difference in your argument?

4. What is chastity? Modesty? What is the difference between them? Is there any connection between them? Would you say that current forms of immodesty in dress cause impurity? As a married person, would you take the view that people become accustomed to what they see and hear in this matter, so that it no longer affects them? Does that hold for adolescents?

5. What is the difference between innocence and ignorance?

6. Why is too much knowledge of sin dangerous? Does this

give you any twinge of conscience concerning the types of newspapers and magazines in your home?

7. Have you ever met the kind of person who boasts about evil things seen or done even though he may never have had these experiences at all? Do not adolescents frequently pretend to know all about sex, when they are actually trying to find out? Do you take for granted that a child who uses knowing terms concerning sex really knows what he is talking about?

8. What is the dual purpose of Christian sex education? Can good sex education ever be made a separate branch of study? Give reasons for your answers.

9. What constitutes a realistic approach to the problems of life? If it views both good and bad, what other element is part of a realistic approach? *(Recognition and acceptance of responsibility.)* Recent wars have shown us three kinds of soldiers. The first kind enlisted with exaggerated and glowing imaginings of the glory and romance of saving their country. The second kind thought only of the sorrow of leaving home and the danger of being wounded or killed. In general, both these types made poor soldiers, and many of them ended in hospital wards for neurotics. The good soldier was the man who, while not ignoring the possible glory involved, knew that war is a messy business, but who recognized his duty and was determined to do it well. What are three similar approaches to marriage; to parenthood?

TRUE OR FALSE?

1. A child can be ignorant and not innocent.

2. A child can be innocent and not ignorant.

3. As far as possible, a young child should be ignorant of sexual sin and crime.

4. A child should be ignorant of all sexual facts.

5. Chastity and modesty are two words for the same thing.

6. A married person can never be chaste.

7. A person living an active married life is not virginal.

8. Immodesty is always a mortal sin.

9. Sex education should be taught as a separate branch of study.

10. Sex education should be woven into the child's general education.

11. A policy of complete silence is the correct approach to sex education.

12. A policy of complete frankness is the best approach to sex education.

13. Realism means being concerned chiefly with evil in life.

Answers: 1—T, 2—T, 3—T, 4—F, 5—F, 6—F, 7—T, 8—F, 9—F, 10—T, 11—F, 12—F, 13—F.

Chapter II

The Church and Sex Education

Exactly what is the attitude of the Church on sex education? Many people, Catholics and non-Catholics alike, say that the Church favors dark ignorance. Others, though they know that this is false, wonder that the Church has not come out with more definite statements on the matter. The dissatisfaction of both sides is due to our American tendency to see things only in black or white. Most Americans rarely make distinctions; they are either for or against a program 100 percent. The Church, on the other hand, is more cautious and examines a program from all sides, and then approves or disapproves with qualifications. The truth of the matter is that the Catholic Church is against the wrong kind of sex education. Toward wholesome sex education she is not merely neutral, she strongly approves! To make this clear, we must glance briefly at some papal pronouncements. We will consider the condemnations of false sex education first, and then go on to consider the approval of correct chastity education.

CONDEMNATIONS

Pope Pius XI, in his encyclical *On the Christian Education of Youth,* says:

> Another very grave danger is that naturalism which nowadays invades the field of education in that most delicate matter of purity of morals. Far too common is the error of those who with dangerous assurance and under

16

an ugly term propagate a so-called sex education, falsely imagining they can forearm youths against the dangers of sensuality by means purely natural, such as a foolhardy initiation and precautionary instruction for all indiscriminately, even in public; and worse still, by exposing them at an early age to the occasions in order to accustom them, so it is argued, and as it were to harden them against such dangers. . . .

In this extremely delicate matter, if, all things considered, some private instruction is found necessary and opportune, from those who hold from God the commission to teach and who have the grace of state, every precaution must be taken.[1]

Here Pius XI is not condemning sex education but "means *purely* natural" (and hence not *all* natural means); "foolhardy initiation"; initiation which is "indiscriminate," that is, not adapted to the needs of the individual and of each sex. He points out that initiation and precautionary instruction (not proper education) are worse if given "even in public." He condemns any effort to harden children by exposing them to temptation. There is a vast difference between condemning such false education and condemning all sex education.[2]

Many modern educators still believe, as the Pope points out, that such false education can prevent sin. They maintain that full knowledge and frequent association with temptation will dull the inclination to evil. Experience abundantly proves that this is not so.

Pope Pius XI also condemns some of the modern forms of preparation for marriage in his encyclical *On Christian Marriage:*

. . . Such wholesome instruction and religious training in regard to Christian marriage will be quite different from that exaggerated physiological education by means of which, in these times of ours, some reformers of married

---

1. Here and elsewhere in this book the encyclicals *On the Christian Education of Youth* and *On Christian Marriage,* and other pronouncements of Pope Pius XI, as well as those of the present Pontiff, are cited in the official N.C.W.C. translations, with the permission of the publisher.
2. For a fuller interpretation of these passages cf. Kirsch, Felix M., O.F.M. Cap., *Sex Education and Training in Chastity* (Benziger Brothers, New York, 1930), pp. xvi-xx.

life make pretense of helping those joined in wedlock, laying much stress on these physiological matters, in which is learned rather the art of sinning in a subtle way than the virtue of living chastely.

Here he condemns *exaggerated* physiological education, not *all* physiological education for the married.

There is one statement of Pius XI above all others that many persons misinterpret:

Hence it is of the highest importance that a good father, while discussing with his son a matter so delicate, be well on his guard and not descend to details, nor refer to the various ways in which this infernal hydra destroys with its poison so large a portion of the world; otherwise it may happen that instead of extinguishing this fire, he unwittingly stirs or kindles it in the simple and tender heart of the child (*On the Christian Education of Youth*).

Some have thought that this forbids the instructor to give the child any physiological information, or to tell him in what the marital act consists. This is not true. Parents should avoid telling the child about the *different sins* that can be committed against sexual morality and about the *circumstances and details* of the marriage act. Nevertheless, "explicit and clear information about the essential character of marital intercourse is not a detail but the very substance of what the parent is setting out to give. The details which the parent is advised to avoid . . . refer to the circumstances accompanying the action."[3]

Therefore the instructor of children must avoid telling the child 1) about all possible sins of impurity, and 2) about all the attendant details or the exact method of performing the marriage act, until such information is necessary. However, at the proper time he may tell the child the precise nature of the marriage act.[4]

---

3. Mahoney, Canon E. J., in the *Clergy Review,* London, March, 1947 (XXVII), p. 194. Quoted with permission of the publisher.
4. Those who are interested in the scientific analysis of official statements may wish to consult: King, J. Leycester, S. J., *Sex Enlightenment and the Catholic* (Burns Oates and Washbourne, London, 1945); also the *Ecclesiastical Review,* June, 1931 (LXXXIV), p. 601, and October, 1931 (LXXXV), pp. 392-395; and the *Clergy Review,* March, 1947 (XXVII), pp. 193-194.

THE CHURCH IN FAVOR OF EDUCATION
FOR CHASTITY

What has the Catholic Church to say in favor of sex education?

1. Pope Pius XI says that such education must be integrated into the education of the whole person, a person raised to the supernatural level:

> In fact it must never be forgotten that the subject of Christian education is man whole and entire, soul united to body in unity of nature, with all his faculties, natural and supernatural, such as right reason and revelation show him to be; man, therefore, fallen from his original estate, but redeemed by Christ and restored to the supernatural condition of adopted son of God, though without the preternatural privileges of bodily immortality or perfect control of appetite. There remain therefore in human nature the effects of original sin, the chief of which are weakness of will and disorderly inclinations. . . . Hence every form of pedagogic naturalism which in any way excludes or weakens supernatural Christian formation in the teaching of youth, is false (*On the Christian Education of Youth*).

2. The Church gives an outline of Christian education to chastity:

> Accordingly special care is to be paid to the complete, solid, and continuous religious instruction of the youth of both sexes; awakening in them a high regard and desire for, and a love of, the angelical virtue; teaching them as a matter of supreme importance to be persevering in prayer, to make assiduous use of the Sacraments of Penance and the Holy Eucharist, to honor the holy purity of the Blessed Virgin Mother with filial devotion, and to commit themselves unreservedly to her protection, teaching them moreover carefully to avoid dangerous reading, indecent scenic performances, wrong conversations and all other occasions of sin. Consequently, works which have recently been written and published, even by certain Catholic authors, advocating a new method of procedure, are in no wise to be approved.[5]

---

5. Decree of the Holy Office, March 21, 1931 (privately translated).

This statement of the Holy Office does not exclude proper sex information, but it insists on the absolutely necessary supernatural basis of Christian education in the matter of purity, together with a realistic approach to original and personal sin and the dangerous occasions of sin.[6]

3. Finally, Pope Pius XII, carefully watching over the families of the world, and mindful of the excessive concern with sex education among modern parents, addressed this clear and magnificent statement to the Women of Catholic Action, representing all the dioceses of Italy, on the feast of Christ the King, October 26, 1941. Here you will find both a justification and an outline of Christian chastity education (italics ours):

Hygiene and Morality	Many of the moral characteristics which you see in the youth or the man owe their origin to the manner and circumstances of his first upbringing in infancy: purely organic habits contracted at that time may later prove a serious obstacle to the spiritual life of the soul. And so you will make it your special care in the treatment of your child to observe the prescriptions of a perfect hygiene, so that when it comes to the use of reason its bodily organs and faculties will be healthy and robust and free from distorted tendencies.
Education to Self-control	. . . From that early age a loving look, a warning word, must teach the child not to yield to all its impressions, and as reason dawns, it must learn to discriminate and to master the vagaries of its sensations; in a word, under the guidance and admonition of the mother it must begin the work of its own education.

6. Cf. comment in *Periodica,* 1931, pp. 243-244.

*Under-
standing
and
Reasoned
Discipline*

Study the child in his tender age. If you know him well you will educate him well; you will not misconceive his character; you will come to understand him, knowing when to give way and when to be firm; a naturally good disposition does not fall to the lot of all the sons of men.

Truth

Train the minds of your children. Do not give them wrong ideas or wrong reasons for things: *whatever their questions may be, do not answer them with evasions or untrue statements,* which their minds rarely accept, but take occasion from them lovingly and patiently to train their minds, which want only to open to the truth and to grasp it with the first ingenuous gropings of their reasoning and reflective powers. . . .

*Adolescence
and Sexual
Stirring*

. . . But the day will come when the childish heart will feel new impulses stirring within it; new desires will disturb the serenity of those early years. In that time of trial, Christian mothers, remember that to train the heart means to train the will to resist the attacks of evil and the insidious temptations of passion; during that period of transition from the unconscious purity of infancy to the triumphant purity of adolescence you have a task of the highest importance to fulfill. You have to prepare your sons and daughters so that they may pass with unfaltering step, like those who pick their way among serpents, through that time of crisis and physical change; and pass through it without losing anything of the joy of innocence, preserving intact that

Modesty:
of Dress
of Action
of Eyes

natural instinct of modesty with which Providence has girt them as a check upon wayward passions. That sense of modesty, which in its spontaneous abhorrence from the impure is akin to the sense of religion, is made of little account in these days; but you, mothers, will take care that they do not lose it through indecency in dress or self-adornment, through unbecoming familiarities or immoral spectacles; on the contrary you will seek to make it more delicate and alert, more

Watchfulness

upright and sincere. You will keep a watchful eye on their steps; you will not suffer the whiteness of their souls to be stained and contaminated by corrupt and corrupt-

Companions

ing company; you will inspire them with a high esteem and jealous love for purity, advising them to commend themselves to

Love of
Purity

the sure and motherly protection of the Immaculate Virgin. Finally, with the discretion of a mother and a teacher, and

Gaining
Confidence

thanks to the openhearted confidence with which you have been able to inspire your children, you will not fail to watch for and

Anticipating
Questions

to discern the moment in which certain *unspoken questions* have occurred to their minds and are troubling their senses. It

Parents
and Sex
Information

will then be *your duty to your daughters, the father's duty to your sons, carefully and delicately to unveil the truth* as far as it appears necessary; to give a *prudent, true and Christian answer* to those questions, and set their minds at rest. If imparted by the lips of Christian parents at the proper time, in the proper measure, and with the proper precautions, the revelation of the mysterious and marvelous

Reverence

laws of life will be received by them with

Less Danger

Evil Sources

reverence and gratitude, and will enlighten their minds; with *far less danger* than if they learned them *haphazard,* from some *unpleasant shock,* from *secret conversations,* through information received from oversophisticated companions, or from clandestine reading, the more dangerous and pernicious as secrecy inflames the imagination and troubles the senses. Your words if they are wise and discreet, will prove a safeguard and a warning in the midst of the temptations and the corruption which surround them, "because foreseen an arrow comes more slowly."[7]

We have presented this statement almost in its entirety in order to convince parents of the stand of the Church on sex education of the right kind. Pius XII talks about hygiene, organic habits in infancy, education in modesty, answering questions truthfully, even anticipating questions, and forestalling smutty information on the matter of purity. This quotation is really an outline of the book you are reading. Study it carefully.

A later statement of Pope Pius XII bears on these matters also. On July 24, 1949, the Pope addressed the women of Italian Catholic Action on matters concerning the Family and Youth. Among other worthwhile things he stressed this admonition: "Educate youth in purity. Help youth when an explaining word of advice and guidance is necessary. Do not forget that a good education must embrace the whole of life and in this sphere especially the habit of self-control is the best formation."[8]

Finally, a very recent address of the Pope to a group of French fathers concerned this same subject, of

7. Translation entitled *Guiding Christ's Little Ones* (N. C. W. C., Washington, D. C., 1942).
8. *Catholic Action,* September, 1949, p. 20. This and all N. C. W. C. material is quoted with permission of the publisher.

chastity education. In the wide publicity accorded this talk by both the Catholic and the secular press, the impression was given that His Holiness was attacking any and all such education. Of course this was not the case. The Holy Father's statements were so forceful that we feel it an obligation to record them, at least in part (italics ours):

> . . . No attempt to influence public opinion ought to be either disdained or neglected.
>
> There is one field in which this education of public opinion, and its correction, has become necessary with tragic urgency. In this field public opinion has been perverted by propaganda that one would not hesitate to call deadly, despite the fact that it comes this time from Catholic sources and seeks to influence Catholics, and even though those who disseminate it do not appear to suspect that they are unknowingly deluded by the spirit of evil.
>
> We are speaking here of the writings, books and articles touching on sexual instruction which today often achieve enormous sales and flood the whole world, engulfing children, submerging the rising generation, and disturbing engaged and newly married couples.
>
> With all the seriousness, attention and dignity the subject requires, the Church has dealt with the question of instruction in this matter *to the extent counseled or demanded* by the *normal physical* and *psychological development* of the adolescent and by *individual cases* arising from varying special circumstances. . . .
>
> This propaganda [of sex education] still threatens Catholics with a double scourge, not to use a stronger term. In the first place, it *exaggerates* beyond all measure the *importance* and *scope* of the *sexual element* in life. Let us grant that these authors, from a purely theoretical point of view, still remain within the limits of Catholic morality; it is nonetheless true that their manner of explaining sexual life is of such a nature as to give it, in the mind of the average reader and in his practical judgment, the *meaning and value of an end in itself.* It makes him lose sight of the true original end of marriage, which is the procreation and education of children, and of the grave duty of married persons toward this end, which the writings about which we are speaking leave too much in the shade.

Secondly, this so-called literature seems to take no account of the general experience of yesterday, today and always, an experience founded on nature which proves that, in moral training neither instruction nor initiation offers any advantage *of itself.* On the contrary, it is seriously unhealthy and prejudicial *unless closely bound to constant discipline, vigorous mastery of oneself,* and above all, the use of supernatural forces—*prayer* and the *Sacraments.* All Catholic teachers worthy of their name and mission are well aware of the preponderant role of supernatural forces in the sanctification of man, be he young or old, bachelor or married. Of these supernatural forces scarcely a word is whispered in the literature of which we speak: they are usually passed over in silence.

The very principles of sexual education and questions related to it, which were so wisely brought forth by Our predecessor Pius XI in his encyclical *Divini Illius Magistri,* are swept aside—sad sign of the times—with a wave of the hand or with a smile. Pius XI, they say, wrote that twenty years ago for his times. We have gone ahead since then.[9]

We have no way of knowing which works Pius XII was referring to in this address. We may presume he had in mind especially some writings in French, since he was speaking to French parents. We can be sure, however, by careful evaluation of his statements that the Pope refers to works: 1) which are written by Catholics; 2) which make of sexual activity an end itself, or which leave in the shade the nature of marriage and its purpose; 3) which do not show proper understanding of the necessity of strong self-discipline, and of frequentation of the Sacraments; and 4) which ignore Pope Pius XI's directions in the encyclical we have already quoted under its English title, *On the Christian Education of Youth.*

The careless reader might infer that His Holiness is attacking all information concerning the nature of the facts of life. This is not so. He tells us that the Church has dealt with such instruction so far as it is

---

9. N. C. W. C. News Service Release, September 28, 1951.

needed by the physical and psychological development of the adolescent, or demanded by special individual circumstances. The preceding quotations in this chapter bear this out in the Pope's own words. True, he says that initiation is of no avail *in itself,* and that it can be harmful; but he adds a strong "unless"—"unless closely bound to constant discipline, etc."

The author humbly submits to the reader that the present work does not fall under the papal strictures. This book does not exaggerate the importance of sex in life; on the contrary, it insists that sex is but one fiber in the total human personality. Sexuality is not treated as an end in itself. Constantly these pages repeat: "Sexual actions are sacred to the married state"; and insist on the vocation of marriage and parenthood with which sex is inextricably bound up. Above all, the pitfall of naturalism has been avoided. Throughout have been stressed the practices of Christian character-building, self-restraint, asceticism, and the frequentation of the Sacraments. The four chapters on religious and moral formation outweigh the physical and psychological chapters in both length and exhaustiveness of treatment; moreover, these four chapters supply the real outline, or "frame of reference," of the entire book. Lastly, the directions of Pope Pius XI have been enshrined in the very first paragraphs of the present chapter.

As you read through the remainder of this book, please refer back constantly to these papal pronouncements, so that you too will avoid the errors and excesses against which His Holiness issues so grave a warning.

There are many more interesting and helpful statements available, but enough have been given to represent the Church's position on this matter. From here on every word of this book will be directed toward explaining the principles of sex education and their application to practical problems.

QUESTIONS AND DISCUSSION AIDS

1. Does the Church condemn sex education? Your answer should start: "It depends on what you mean by sex education. . . ."

2. Can you list any dangers in the approach through means "purely natural"? through "precautionary instruction for all indiscriminately, even in public"? Does this forbid all precautionary instruction? Will exposure to temptation harden people to it?

3. Who are "those who hold the commission from God to teach and have the grace of state"? (Save your answer for future reference in Chapter III.)

4. Is every kind of physiological instruction forbidden to married persons or persons about to be married? What kind is condemned?

5. What two things are forbidden by the statement of the Pope that the parent "should . . . not descend to details, nor refer to the various ways this infernal hydra destroys . . . so large a portion of the world"?

6. Why is the Church so anxious for the use of positive supernatural helps and a positive approach to purity?

7. Pick out the sentences and phrases which seem most important in the statement of Pope Pius XII to mothers. Discuss them.

8. Why is the Pope's statement so valuable? (Consider the grace given to him as head of the Church; his concern for the good of all; his expert advisers, etc.)

Chapter III

Whose Duty is Sex Education?

INSTRUCTION AND EDUCATION IN SEX MATTERS MUST
BE GIVEN BY PARENTS OR THEIR DELEGATES

The parents have the primary right and the duty to educate their children. Since, as we have shown, sex education is merely a part of general education, the primary right and duty of parents extends also to sex education.

Pope Pius XI states, in the encyclical *On the Christian Education of Youth:*

> The family therefore holds directly from the Creator the mission and hence the right to educate the offspring, a right inalienable because inseparably joined to the strict obligation, a right anterior to any right whatever of civil society and of the State, and therefore inviolable on the part of any power on earth. . . .

The wisdom of the Church in this matter is expressed with precision and clearness in the Code of Canon Law, Canon 1113: "Parents are under a grave obligation to see to the religious and moral education of their children, as well as to their physical and civil training, as far as they can. . . ."

28

PARENTS HAVE THE SERIOUS OBLIGATION IN CONSCIENCE TO GIVE THE NECESSARY SEX INSTRUCTION AND EDUCATION

Parents above all others have the commission from God to teach children. They also have the special graces of their state. One of the graces they receive with the Sacrament of Matrimony *is the supernatural help to educate their children.* If parents feel that they are not prepared to meet their obligations in the matter of sex education, *it is their duty to prepare themselves.* The author has yet to meet the father or mother who could not supply their children's needs if they made an effort. A great deal of schooling is not necessary, though it may be helpful. The requirements are a small but correct vocabulary, a sensible and Christian attitude, and an understanding of principles and of children. Pope Pius XII is very explicit on the duty of parents to be educators, and on their duty to prepare themselves for this task:

> We need not delay to remind you how important and how necessary is this work of education in the home, and how grave a mother's obligation not to neglect it or perform it with indifference. . . . This obligation [is] the first of their duties as Christian mothers, and . . . a task in which none can fully take their place. But it is not enough to be conscious of an obligation and to have the desire to discharge it; it is necessary also to render oneself capable of discharging it competently.[1]

Some parents shirk the duty of chastity education for one of two reasons. They do not know the correct words to use, or they feel such an emotional disturbance over the subject that they cannot bring themselves to talk to their children about it.[2]

Few technical words are required—fewer by far than are included in this study. Wrong attitudes are more difficult to correct, but they can be overcome with effort.

---

1. *Guiding Christ's Little Ones*, p. 2.
2. Cf. Fleege, Urban H., *Self-Revelation of the Adolescent Boy* (Bruce, Milwaukee, 1945), p. 275.

As a matter of fact, however, parents are educating their children whether they intend to or not. Children imbibe their parents' attitudes toward politics, race relations, honesty, patriotism, and so on. Attitudes on sex are no exception to this generally acknowledged fact. The minds, attitudes, and moral habits of children are plastic. They can be shaped in almost the same way as wax is shaped in molds. If the mold supplied in the home is good, their formation will be good. But if parents have no definite ideas on this matter, no definite mold to give, their children will be shaped poorly. Positive education forms the child; negative education allows the child to be formed by someone else. Therefore, either your child will adopt your attitude (whether of shamefaced silence, brash frankness, or wholesome reverence) or he will go elsewhere for his formation. He may receive it from playmates, random (and often evil) reading, older meddlers, movies, etc. And what he does not learn from these sources he may learn from actual experimentation.

One sometimes hears parents say: "My children do not need any instruction from me. They learn all they need to know from the movies, newspapers, magazines, advertisements, etc." This do-nothing attitude is disastrous. Even if children did learn the important facts of life from such sources, are they wholesome sources? *It is not so much the learning of the physiological facts that matters, but rather the children's attitudes and judgments on these facts.*

It is our opinion, however, that children and adolescents do not get correct information even from these sources. They are merely inspired to try to find out what is behind the things that seem to tell them so much. Their curiosity is stirred. Their appetites begin to trouble them even though they do not know what it is all about. They observe that near-nudity is common; that immodesty in dress is widely held to be necessary for "glamour" and popularity; they come to think that love consists in mere bodily attraction and emotional romance. Some adolescents start to practice the love-making techniques they see on the screen. The very fact that children are faced with all these influences makes it imperative that parents engage in positive education on all phases of chastity and modesty.

There are two things, above all others, which parents must do in the face of the pagan atmosphere in which their children live. *First, they must constantly observe and judge the influences that affect their children.* If they do not, they will find themselves adopting some of the world's false attitudes. The eminent philosopher Dr. Yves Simon expresses the opinion that the constant impact of propaganda and advertising on uncritical minds acts like a blackjack. After a time, such propaganda can make men slaves more effectively than the lash.[3] *Second, parents must gradually teach their children to judge these influences.* This *does not* mean that parents should at once point out to their children all the evils in the world, for this might stir up passion unnecessarily. At first, their teaching should be of such a kind that the child will apply it unconsciously to what he sees and hears. Then, in later adolescence, boys and girls may well be taught to pass accurate and explicit judgments on these influences.

As a last incentive for parents to assume this important task, let them consider the following facts. In a study of 2,000 Catholic boys in Catholic high schools (and therefore presumably under the best possible influence), it was found that unwholesome sources of sex information outnumbered wholesome sources three to one. When brought to bear, many of the wholesome sources were as much as six years too late.[4] These figures are conservative. Other authors put the unwholesome sources much higher. There can be no doubt, then,

---

3. *The Nature and Function of Authority* (Marquette University Press, Milwaukee, 1940), pp. 55ff.
4. Cf. Fleege, *op. cit.*, pp. 272-274, 276.

that the chastity of children depends on the education given them by their parents. This education is a serious and primary obligation of parents.

DELEGATES

It may happen that parents are not equipped to give the proper instruction in sex, and that before they can prepare themselves to do so, some such instruction is needed by their children. In such a case, the parents must choose a substitute or delegate. They may choose a priest or nun, the family doctor, a nurse, a relative who is qualified, a school teacher. These substitutes cannot completely supply for the parents in sex *education,* though they may supply for one or the other sex *instruction* (for example, at the age of 12 or 14). After all, the parent knows the child better than anyone else, and has a continuous contact with him.

Besides, each of the delegates listed suffers under several disadvantages. The doctor or nurse tends to be too physiological and medical. The priest or nun may find it difficult to win the confidence of the child because of their position of authority. All substitutes are hampered by lack of time and the difficulty of sufficiently understanding the child's background. Certainly, a mother with five children has many more opportunities to gain knowledge of her children and win their confidence than a school teacher with 40 children, or a priest who must care for 1,000. However, when it is really necessary for the good of the child, any one of these substitutes may give the needed instruction. Parents, priests and teachers, both lay and religious, all have a "commission to teach and a grace of state."[5]

The Priest in the Confessional

It has sometimes been said that sex instruction can best be accomplished by the priest in the confessional.

5. Cf. also, Kirsch, *op. cit.,* p. 164.

There are many reasons why this opinion is false. First of all, the priest very often has no opportunity to instruct until sin, or even a habit of sin, is brought to his attention. Then it is so late that his instruction in the confessional can be merely corrective. Second, there is the time element; the priest cannot risk the child's resentment at being detained too long, or the child's fear of drawing the attention of his companions or parents waiting outside. Third, the confessional is dark, so that the priest cannot see and be guided by the reactions of the child. Fourth, even were instruction attempted in the confessional, so much would have to be given at one time that a great deal of it would be missed by the child, or immediately forgotten. For these reasons and many others, it is the author's opinion that the only effective sex instruction the priest can give in the confessional is that concerning the morality of certain acts. He can do much remedial work, but little of a positive nature.[6]

Outside the confessional, of course, the priest may be very helpful. His work in the school and in personal interviews is of great assistance in these matters. Some adolescents prefer to talk over their sexual problems with a priest because his celibate life gives him a more objective and impersonal view of the whole realm of chastity, in or out of marriage.[7]

Tacit and Express Delegation

It is not necessary that parents expressly choose those who substitute for them in giving sex instructions. If the parents have not won the confidence of the child in this matter, they will not know when he is in need of help. Teachers are assistants to the parents in the work of educating children, and there is no reason why they may not give a certain amount of sex

---

6. Further reasons against instruction in the confessional can be found in the Code of Canon Law, Canon 888, § 2; cf. also the Private Response of the Sacred Office, May 16, 1943, in regard to treating these matters in the confessional.
7. Cf. Kirsch, *op. cit.,* pp. 116, 163; Fleege, *op. cit.,* pp. 276-277.

instruction to their charges according to *individual* needs. (They should never attempt this, it goes without saying, unless they are reasonably sure that the child needs some instruction, and that he is not getting it at home.)

This holds, in fact, for all qualified persons who are spontaneously approached by a child. Such approach does not necessarily mean that the child asks a point-blank question; he may merely give various indirect indications, references, etc., which hint of his need. It is right to answer his appeal, for the reason that the parents may be presumed to be reasonably willing to have the child's needs met by a really competent instructor. In the case of a child and a close Catholic relative or Catholic teacher, the parents' willingness would seem unquestionable. Such willingness could hardly be presumed in the case of persons more casually connected with the child.

Note, however, that the individual who undertakes such a task assumes serious responsibilities. He must not merely *feel* capable. There are too many who undertake to instruct children when they are less qualified than the children themselves. They must be reasonably assured of their ability chastely to educate or instruct a child. One who has mastered the contents of this book or a similar work may consider himself qualified. But even doctors or nurses, if they merely know the physiology of sex but have not formed *proper attitudes* for themselves, are not capable of educating others.

There should be a dependable norm for the Catholic doctor, nurse, social worker, or school teacher who may read this work. *Those who are in a position to gain the confidence of the child, who are properly qualified in language, Catholic principles and attitudes, whom the child spontaneously approaches, may, upon realizing the need of the child and its lack of instruction at home, reasonably presume the consent of the parents to give some instruction.* This instruction may supplement parental education or even supply for it if necessary.

No parents who read the section above should use it as an excuse for not educating their own children in this matter. At the very best, instructors other than parents make poor substitutes for the work of the home. Most of them have no strict obligation to undertake the task, while the parents have such an obligation. Besides, as will be repeatedly pointed out, education in this matter should take in the whole growing life of the child. The parents alone are in contact with the child over the whole period.

THE PLACE OF THE CATHOLIC DOCTOR, NURSE, PSYCHIATRIST, ETC.

A group of parents will do well to become acquainted with a Catholic doctor, nurse, psychiatrist, child specialist, etc., whom they can consult if special problems arise. Such consultation might be necessary in the case of a child who reacts wrongly to instruction, or who contracts a bad habit, for example, masturbation. The specialists will be helpful, but they should be Catholic if at all possible. We do not mean merely specialists who are Catholic, but *truly Catholic specialists,* that is, those who practice their profession according to Catholic moral principles. Priests can frequently help in directing parents to such doctors, etc.

MOTHER OR FATHER?

Both mother and father have the obligation of educating their child to a chaste life. They are meant to be of mutual help, in this problem as in all others. In actual instruction, the father is obviously the "natural" one for the boys, the mother for the girls. However, it will be found at times that the mother is the better instructor for both sons and daughters until puberty or beyond. (This age varies with individuals, but is usually considered to be about 14 for boys and 12 for girls.)

No father should interpret what is said here as freeing him from responsibility in the sex education of his children. A good norm is: *Whichever parent is asked, should answer.*

QUESTIONS AND DISCUSSION AIDS

1. Who has the right to educate a child? Who has the duty? Would the willful omission of this duty constitute a serious sin?

2. Why are parents alone in a position to give really adequate sex education?

3. Who or what is actually forming the mind of your children on sexual matters: You? The school? Your children's friends? Magazines? Comic books? Obscene pictures? Have you ever attempted to find out?

4. As an exercise in judgment, pick up any secular magazine and turn to a modern love story. Read it. Is the heroine's physical beauty described in excessive detail? Are passionate scenes presented? Does the author linger on such detail? Is there one incident in which the heroine disrobes or appears in a bathing suit? If so, has the illustrator selected this one (perhaps passing) incident for his illustration? Has the incident any real connection with the story? If not, why do you think it was introduced? Do hero and heroine marry within two weeks or less? Is divorce involved? Is there any mention of parenthood or children? Granting even that one or another story of this kind might be harmless, could a steady diet of such reading be healthy? In the same magazine count the advertisements. How many say in every line: "Romance, glamour, passion, can be had if you buy, wear, use, this product"?

Consider this cynical quotation from a story in a popular magazine: "Burlesque isn't dead, it's only been transferred to magazine illustrations." Would you consider this statement true?

Judge the last movie you saw in the light of its effect: 1) on young children; 2) on adolescents. Will these influences be the ones that educate your children? How can you combat them?

5. If you have adolescent girls, do you face any problems in persuading them to choose modest costumes, bathing suits, etc.? If so, has their judgment been warped by their surroundings? How can you help them to judge what is modest?

6. Can anyone but a father or mother really supply all parental instruction? In cases of necessity who may supplement the work of parents?

7. Should the father or the mother be the one to instruct the children in sex?

Chapter IV

General Norms For Sex Education

SEX EDUCATION MUST BE GRADUAL

Many people are surprised to hear that sex education must be gradual. They think of fulfilling this task in one "heart-to-heart talk." Popular literature has confirmed this error by referring to the "birds and bees" lecture that parents are to give their children. This is against good common sense, for no child learns anything completely in one lesson. When a child of six asks what makes the train go, do you try to explain all the mechanical working of a steam engine? No, you answer simply, "Steam," and let it go at that. Again, the same subjects, to a large degree, are taught in grade school, high school, and college, simply because human beings learn gradually. The process is the same for sex education, but with an added reason. The child's sexual passions must not be awakened too soon. It must always be remembered that:

> There remain . . . in human nature the effects of original sin, chief of which are weakness of will and disorderly inclinations.[1]

It is foolish to try to teach the young child some things, such as higher mathematics, because he will not be able to grasp them. It is foolish to teach him the facts about sex too soon, not only because his understanding is weak, but because he may learn enough to exper-

---

1. Pius XI, *On the Christian Education of Youth.*

iment with his own passions. Do not object that this premature awakening is impossible. Statistics are on hand that would make you shudder.

Shock

Another reason for making sex education a gradual process is the danger of shocking a child. The nature of emotional shock must be understood. A shock is produced by a sudden and disagreeable surprise. We are shocked, for example, at the unexpected announcement of a good friend's death. We are not shocked at a pleasant surprise, though we may be amazed. Again, if a disagreeable fact comes upon us not suddenly, but gradually, we may be saddened, but we are not shocked. To take examples: we are *shocked* when a well-mannered child suddenly and convincingly cries, "I hate you"; we are pleasantly *amazed* when a moderately talented child suddenly takes all honors; we are *saddened* at a child who sins seriously, for to anyone who realizes the weakness of human nature, sin, however disagreeable, can never be a surprise.

Now, shock for a child in sexual matters usually has the two elements, of *sudden surprise* over a *disagreeable fact*. For example, it happened once that a boy of nine, totally unprepared, came upon a picture series in a doctor's book explaining a Caesarian birth. Naturally, he thought it the only method of birth. He was shocked at the sudden "knowledge" that his mother had to go through a terrible operation to give him life. If the instruction and education of a child are gradual, there will be no surprise, and the disagreeableness will be lessened. (The specific approach for eliminating any disagreeable effect of such information will be treated later.)

A still further reason for gradual education is the nature of the child's questions and curiosity. A child's first questions are ontological, not sexual. By this is meant that the child is interested in the world of things that exist, especially in living things. He is not sexually preoccupied. He is not searching for pleasure, nor is he interested in the mechanics of generation. He simply wants to know what things are, why they exist, and where they came from. Later on he will become curious about bodily mechanisms and pleasures. Naturally, then, you answer the questions that interest him and no more. A young child may be interested enough to ask where the new baby came from, but he or she will not ordinarily be concerned with how it got out, or how it came to be there in the first place. Therefore you instruct a child simply in the order of its need.

SEX EDUCATION SHOULD BE PRIVATE

The general rule of "privacy" for sex education applies chiefly to instruction on the intimate facts about sex, and to those portions of the child's training that are liable to be the more stimulating, such as warnings on venereal disease, explanations on how to act in a bathroom, and cautions against sinful actions. This does not mean that every child must always be instructed in such things individually, though frequently that is the best method. "Private" here means that instruction must be adapted to the personal needs of each child. Children in a family within a certain age range may often be instructed together.

Private instruction is important for two reasons: first, because of the child's psychological make-up; and second, because of the impossibility of meeting the needs of individuals in group instruction.

It must be understood that sexual instruction is liable to be stirring if presented vividly, or if several persons are present, or if it is given to a group of both sexes. Anyone who has ever talked to boys or girls on the subject, even in the most general terms, will bear this out. One who has gained a boy's or girl's confidence can talk to the child alone very easily. But an instructor who addresses a group of both boys and girls on anything pertaining to sex can almost feel the tension among them.

Of course broader educational points can be made to a group consisting of both sexes. This is the function of the school. General right attitudes toward marriage and parenthood can be fostered by the use of examples from history and literature, by analyzing the home life of foreign peoples, by suggestions in home economics and manual training classes and in religion courses. The priest can and should preach on the larger moral problems pertaining to chastity, matrimony, vocation, etc. However, intimate facts and delicate personal adjustments must always be left for private interviews. The common moral principles can be taught in the school, but the personal applications should be made in the home, in the confessional, or in other person-to-person contacts.

Mothers and fathers should create occasions when their children can talk to them of *all* their problems, not only the sex problem. If that is the practice in a home, sex problems will be easily proposed. The hour when the children are taking or being given a bath offers a good opportunity for some instruction to those who are very young. There are other made-to-order occasions, as when the mother is helping a child to dress, or combing its hair, or doing a chore with the help of the child. Hikes, fishing jaunts, co-operation in a hobby, even lesson time, all provide good occasions for a father to talk over problems with his son. No matter how busy or how large a household, opportunities can be found for those brief private chats that are so valuable a means of education in all spheres.

Sex Education Must Be Repeated

Parents are sometimes amazed to learn that repetition is needed in sex education and instruction. They think that once the inevitable questions are asked and answered, their troubles are at an end. Children forget; sometimes, indeed, their minds are distracted even while you are instructing them. Children learn few things "all at once." Did your child learn the multiplication table at one sitting? Was a single lesson enough to teach it obedience, or honesty, or any virtue? Of course not. Sex education is no different. Convictions and habits are built up only over a long period of time. It requires many admonitions and instructions, backed by constant good example, to make a mature person out of your child. If he comes to you with a question on sex that you answered before and shows no recollection of the answer, it may actually be a good sign. It may mean that the child is not mulling too much over these matters; and it also shows that the child has such confidence in you that he is not worrying that needed knowledge will be withheld. Only if the child returns frequently and at brief intervals with questions about sex, or if there is some indication that he is overly anxious, will it be necessary to caution him about too much thought on the subject.

There may come a time when your child needs a review of all that you have said over a long period. This is natural, and you should not be surprised at it. It seems to the writer that this is about the only time when a complete booklet will be useful for a boy or girl. For those of the age of, say, 15 or 16, a good booklet may put into final order the instructions you have given over a period of years. The same booklet, however, might be dangerous if you have avoided all previous informal education. Should you decide to give such a book to your child, first read it yourself to find out whether, in your judgment, it fits that child's need.

SEX EDUCATION MUST BE CONTINUED THROUGHOUT THE
PERIOD OF GROWTH

If sex education is to be gradual, private, repeated and reviewed, then it will take a long time. It should be spread over a lifetime, from birth through maturity.

Education will continue for a lifetime, but parental duties will be over or nearly over by the time one's child is about 18. The truth must be told the child at every age, but not always *all* the truth. Bits of knowledge should fit themselves into the child's mind so imperceptibly that he will not notice how much he is learning. If a child is trained in this way, then when the time of full enlightenment arrives, the information will seem natural, unspectacular, and even "old stuff."

It would be well if we lived in a society in which children could reach maturity, and find it economically possible to marry at an earlier age. In such a society, mature sex education could be reached by the age of 17 and marriage soon afterward. The world in which we actually live creates sex interest and problems at an early age and yet makes impossible the normal solution of such problems by an early marriage. That is why we state that sex education should last from 3 to 18. Adjustment to problems arising from that point until marriage is a special field that needs more attention from Catholic writers.

Instruction Must Meet and Slightly Anticipate the Needs of the Individual

Everyone will agree that education should meet the needs of each individual, and enable him to meet and solve successfully the problems of real life. However, it is difficult to judge what is the proper time for certain instructions. For example, generally speaking, a boy should have definite information shortly before his first seminal emission; a girl, shortly before her first menstruation. But when will this happen to a particular child? You cannot foresee the exact time. Therefore, the child should be prepared in a general way in advance, so that when the time comes he or she will recall something of what has been said and have confidence enough to come back and ask for a more complete explanation. In other words, one instruction will be given before the need arises, another afterward. The first instruction will not be fully understood because there is no experience behind it. After the first experience, a more complete instruction can be given with a better chance of understanding.

Precisely When?

This is a difficult question to answer. There are seldom two children of the same physical constitution in the same family. One authority states that most girls experience their first menstruation at the age of 13 years and 9 months, and that most boys experience seminal emission for the first time at about 14 years and 6 months. Yet no hard-and-fast date can be set down. There are many preliminary signs of puberty. When the youngsters begin to grow rapidly out of their clothes, when the boy's voice begins to change and he shows signs of a mustache, when the girl's breasts begin to develop and her figure changes from angles to curves, puberty is fast approaching. Certainly, when the mother notes a stain on the child's bed clothing or pajamas, the full instructions for puberty should be given.

When should the preliminary instruction be given? A good norm is, about 2 years before the age of puberty: thus, about the eleventh year for the girl and the twelfth for the boy. However, there is one fact of modern life that may make it necessary to give a boy or girl an even earlier instruction on bodily organs and changes. Children talk a great deal among themselves. Various studies which have been made concerning their first knowledge of the sexual mechanism, show this. According to Fleege,[2] 68 percent of the boys studied received enlightenment from companions in the seventh grade, and most girls learn the facts about sex in the sixth grade. It therefore seems safe to recommend

---

2. *Op. cit.*, p. 276.

that the first rather complete instruction be given to boys entering the seventh grade, and to girls entering the sixth.

Someone may say: "Well, if some learn even earlier, then we should give an earlier instruction to all." The answer is, that in dealing with human things we cannot prepare for every possible problem. If some children learn at 7, should we teach them *all* at 6? No; the dangers attached to premature enlightenment by parents outweigh the chances of the child's being informed from other sources at an early age. Moreover, the danger can be greatly lessened where the parents so win the confidence of the child that he will come to them if he receives any sex information elsewhere. *If, however, the child has actually received information from unwholesome sources, correct information must be imparted at once.*

The twofold instruction spoken of above—that is, both before and after the need has declared itself—applies to other things besides seminal emission and menstruation. Such occasions are: the first appearance of attraction to the opposite sex; the first temptations against purity; the more difficult dangers when the adolescent goes off to work, or to college, or into nurses training; the dangers in boy-and-girl relationships; and finally, the beginning of company-keeping.

Forewarned is forearmed. Yet the forewarning must not take the form of vivid imaginative descriptions. Instead, this preliminary instruction should be general and more or less technical in terminology, and should appeal to the reason rather than to the imagination. It should be such that when, *but only when,* a temptation or bodily reaction is experienced, it will be recognized for what it is. Then the second and more complete instruction will be in order.

QUESTIONS AND DISCUSSION AIDS

1. List several common-sense reasons why sex education should be gradual. What two elements enter into shock? Do you think both elements can be eliminated in sex education? Could they be at least softened?

2. What does the element of privacy mean in Christian sex education? Why should personal adjustments be private? Must each and every element of sex education be imparted in private? From the material contained in this and the previous chapter, what reasons must be opposed to formal sex education in the school?

3. Is it sufficient to take a child aside for just one talk on the whole subject of sex? Why are repetition and review necessary? Draw some parallels from other problems in life (for example, preparing for an examination, making a retreat, checking over your financial standing, etc.).

4. Try to formulate some answers to a child's first curious questions about babies. Save your ideas for comparison with what you will learn in Chapter XI.

5. At what time in a child's life should some instruction on sexual facts certainly be given? Can a definite time be assigned that applies equally to all?

6. What factors might make it necessary to give a child certain information earlier than the general norms indicate?

7. Discuss this quotation: "Talks should be held in strict secrecy between father and son or mother and daughter. They will definitely be justified and directly beneficial for they will correspond to the natural awakening of sex in the young person. At this time, such conversations cannot be harmful, since parents and children already understand that the subject is secret and important and must be discussed to obtain benefits which, remaining intimate, will equally be real. . . . Such talks must also cover sex hygiene and particularly questions of sexual morality."

Do you think this quotation must be one from a Catholic source? As a matter of fact it is a verbatim translation of a directive of the Soviet government on sex education![3] Can you believe that this comes from a government which once advocated the most frank forms of sexual initiation? Will the knowledge of this about-face after years of experience make you wary of sex education proposals in the schools? Why?

---

3. Cf. *U. S. News and World Report* (independent weekly news magazine, Washington, D. C.), July 22, 1949, p. 26: "Russia Takes a New Line on Sex." Quoted with permission of the copyright owner.

Chapter V

Religious Content of
Catholic Sex Education: I

(VOCATION, SEX, AND THE PURPOSE OF LIFE)

What should be contained in a complete Catholic education on sex? It is hard to separate the elements of sex education from general education; and this is exactly the reason why sex education itself should *not be separated* from general education. However, for purposes of study we shall attempt to outline the content of Catholic education to chastity. The remainder of the book is concerned with this content material.

Catholic sex education should be religious, moral, emotional, psychological and physiological, and in that order of importance. It should also embrace **warnings of danger** and give a **remote and proximate preparation for marriage.** It is difficult to separate these elements. Indeed, just as sex education should not be separated from general education, so each of these elements of sex education should not be separated from the others. It is a natural thing to blend them together. For example, who would wish to separate the noble emotion of real love from the religious fact that in marriage husband and wife symbolize the union of Christ with His Church?

It is necessary, moreover, to take special care *never* to separate physiological information from an emotional, ethical or religious viewpoint. Never say, "This organ is called this, and is used in this way." Indicate the

48

moral meaning of its use, or the wonder of the power of procreation, or parallel the information with the Hail Mary, etc.

PURPOSE OF MAN

So much of our religion affects our outlook on sex that there is room here to sketch out only the most important truths and attitudes. You are placed on this earth to know, love and serve God. You are not here primarily to be a dictator, to make money, or have fun. You know and love God by your intellect and will, and supernaturally by the virtues of faith, hope and charity. How do you serve Him? You serve God by keeping His laws and *by performing the duties of your state in life* to the best of your ability. It makes no difference what position you hold, whether president or porter; it makes no difference what your state of life is, married, single, or vowed to God's service. You can only reach God by carrying out your particular duties to the best of your ability according to His law.

STATE OF LIFE

There are three general states or vocations in life: the conjugal or married state, the state of virginity in the world, and the state of virginity in a religious order or the priesthood.

Virginity

If we forget for a moment the circumstances affecting this or that individual, and examine the states of life *in themselves,* virginity is the higher state *when embraced for a supernatural reason.* Speaking of a father's duty toward an unmarried daughter, St. Paul says: "He who gives his virgin in marriage does well, and he who does not give her does better" (*1 Cor.* 7:38). Notice that St. Paul says virginity is better—he does not say marriage is sinful! In fact, he denies that strongly: "If thou takest a wife, thou hast not sinned. And if a virgin marries, she has not sinned" (*1 Cor.* 7:28). His distinction is between what is *good* and what is *better.*

Why is virginity better? The state of virginity makes it possible for the individual to love God more *directly* without distraction (cf. *1 Cor.* 7:25-35). Virginity gives a person an opportunity to sacrifice himself by completely overcoming the drive of bodily passion. This state is a more difficult life in many ways, and *if chosen out of love of God,* is more meritorious. When consecrated by the vows of religion, virginity becomes even more noble.

However, if a man or woman were to embrace celibacy or virginity for merely selfish motives, to avoid responsibility, to have ease and comfort, etc., his or her virginity would be far less noble than marriage. St. Augustine states this pungently:

> Virginity is not honored because it is virginity, but because it is dedicated to God![1]

Clerical and Cloistered Virginity

How many thousands of young men and women have gone into the priesthood and cloister to serve God and neighbor with all their strength! They are the silent heroes of every age in history. They have bound up the spiritual and physical wounds of mankind. They have brought sinful men back to God. Throughout the centuries they have been for human society the nurses, the educators, the librarians, the experimental farmers, the scientists and inventors, as well as the mystics and contemplatives. Their contribution to the good of man can never be measured in terms of dollars and cents, for without their efforts culture and Christian civilization itself might be dead. Priests and religious give the lie

---

1. *On Virgins,* chapter 8.

to the pagan claim, heard so often, that continence is impossible, or if possible, fruitless. Such men and women give fully of their lives, and ask only "food and sufficient clothing, with these . . . [they are] content" (*1 Tim.* 6:8). Here is a worthy vocation in life, a career that cannot be equaled by any worldly calling.

Virginity in the World

Virginity, as has been said, is a state of life possible not only in the cloister but also outside it. Many of our young people are following this state in the world with a very holy purpose. Many nurses, social workers, doctors, teachers and hundreds of others have voluntarily embraced virginity to devote themselves to their work and through their work to God. If anyone doubts the worth of such a sacrifice, let him consult Pope Pius XII's statement in *Women's Duties in Social and Political Life.*[2]

Matrimony

The third noble state of life is the conjugal state. "Marriage is the lawful contract between man and woman by which is given and accepted the exclusive and perpetual right to those mutual bodily functions which are naturally apt to generate offspring."[3] Stated in these cold words, marriage does not seem to mean much. But for baptized Christians, it is far more. Christ has raised this natural contract to the dignity and holiness of a Sacrament. Through it He grants to the spouses all the graces needed for their heavy duties, and He renders their contract, already permanent by natural law, absolutely unbreakable in life. As He Himself says: "Now they are no longer two, but one flesh. What therefore God has joined together, let no man put asunder" (*Mark* 10:8-9). The wonderful and uniquely personal

2. Paulist Press, New York, 1945.
3. Davis, *op. cit.*, Vol. IV, p. 53.

thing about this Sacrament is that the bride and groom are the ministers of it. The priest does not confer the Sacrament, he is merely the official witness at the ceremony. Husband and wife confer the Sacrament on each other with all its graces. Not only do they give each other their bodies and their lives, but they also give to each other the Sacrament from which come the graces needed to perform their duties. By performing these duties properly, they gain Heaven. In the Sacrament of Matrimony, therefore, there are only three actors: a man, a woman, and—no, not a priest but—God!

SEX AND MARRIAGE

Sex acts are sacred and reserved to the married. Though the human sexual functions are indeed physical, and similar to those of animals (note we say *similar,* not the same by any means), a man and woman co-operate not merely in the production of a body, but toward the creation of *a human person,* who has a soul. It is God alone who produces the soul; but parents are co-creators with Him in bringing the whole person into existence. The human child is not a little animal that merely eats and drinks and grows up to reproduce his kind. He is a person: a being of tremendous worth. He thinks, he wills, he loves, he becomes responsible for his acts. He can know and love God, and with supernatural help he can reach Heaven; that is, he can attain such a state of perfection that he is able to participate in the Life of God.

A human being is valuable—so valuable that God Himself saw fit to unite a human nature with His Divine nature in the Person of Christ. If a human person is sacred as a result of such consecration by God, then the act by which he is produced, the sexual act of husband and wife, is sacred and holy; because if an effect is holy, its cause must be holy.

The highest appreciation the non-Christian can have of marriage is that it builds up the human race. The desire to perfect the human race by bringing children into the world, and by bringing them to the highest perfection, is very noble. Yet how much more noble it is to have the vocation of building up the Mystical Body of Christ, to help extend Christ's holy Body, the Church, to the ends of the earth!

The humblest of laboring men should regard his home life as an apostolate out of which Church and nation may draw the priests, missionaries and apostles they need. For the basic ideal of family life is to "multiply the number of the elect." Let this be brought home to the working classes, for they in particular are equal to the acts of generosity, devotion and self-denial which such an ideal demands. And it is the proper development of the worker's family life in accordance with this ideal that must be kept in mind when facing questions such as the living wage, the housing problem, married women workers, and that of supply and demand in economics; and also in fighting the liberalism and individualism, and the "statism," collectivism, and materialistic nationalism which are its enemies. Family life inspired by this high ideal affords a proper basis for the decent education and moral training of the young. It gives a truly supernatural foundation to their courtships and their friendships, which alone is able to withstand the teaching and morals of modern paganism.[4]

The nobility of marriage is further shown by the fact that St. Paul uses the union of husband and wife as a miniature or symbol of the mystical union of Christ with His Church (*Eph.* 5:22-32):

Let wives be subject to their husbands as to the Lord; because a husband is the head of the wife, just as Christ is head of the Church. . . .

---

4. Canon Cardijn, *The Spirit of the Y.C.W.* (Catholic Truth Society, Toronto, 1940), pp. 13-14. Quoted with permission of the publisher.

Husbands, love your wives, just as Christ also loved the Church. . . . He who loves his own wife, loves himself. For no one ever hated his own flesh; on the contrary he nourishes and cherishes it, as Christ also does the Church (because we are members of His body, made from His flesh and from His bones).

"For this cause a man shall leave his father and mother and cleave to his wife; and the two shall become one flesh."

This is a great mystery—I mean in reference to Christ and to the Church.

PURPOSES OF MARRIAGE

For many moderns, the purposes of marriage are the gratification and pleasure of the couple. Children, when they are thought of, come last in their plans. We sometimes wonder whether such couples ever desire children except as an expression of their own selfishness. In any event, their wish for children never rises above the merely natural level. Some want a boy or girl, not for the child's sake, but for their own. They want someone to love, and someone to show off. They want the pleasure of association with the child, perhaps even some companionship in their old age—a few children are a good investment! So long as their comfort, freedom or pleasure is not hindered, they will have a few— and only a few. They feel no sense of vocation to raise a family for itself.

This attitude is very incomplete. Few of those who have it would admit it even to themselves, for in many cases it is unconscious. Nevertheless, the fact is there. True, all the joys they wish from their children can be justly sought, but such happiness should be a *result* of their vocation as parents, not the prime purpose of their married lives.

How different is the Catholic concept! The first purpose of marriage is children. To beget and educate children is a career that should stimulate work and sacrifice. The second purpose of marriage is mutual love, help and service, not only in bodily and temporal needs, but also in spiritual things. Married Christians must seek God *together.* The last, but by no means unimportant, purpose is to provide a legitimate and holy outlet for concupiscence. We must not lose sight of the order of purposes within the marriage state.

VOCATIONS AND SEX EDUCATION

Why all this material on states of life when we are speaking of sex education? Is it not a disgression? No. *Sexual acts and sexual pleasure are reserved for the married.* (This should be repeated again and again.) If this is true, then a mature outlook on the use of sex depends on one's choice of a state of life. Once the individual has finally chosen, that state is the way to Heaven for him. All discussion concerning the relative value of the different states in life ceases when that decision is made, for in the concrete, the best vocation for each person is the one to which he is called.[5] Obviously then, a part of sex education is an understanding of states in life. We can never integrate attitudes on sex into our lives until we understand where sexual activity belongs.

The Child and Vocation

All three states of life should be frequently presented to the child for consideration. He should be told that he is free to choose the married state, virginity in the world, or virginity in the cloister or in the priesthood.

---

5. This does not mean that once a choice has been made it cannot be changed. Up until the time of Ordination, final vows, or wedding day, the decision may be revoked. This holds also for the state of virginity in the world. Mature decision may change an early attraction to any one state. Adolescents should not be accused of fickleness if they change their minds as they grow older.

Since each state is a vocation from God, the child should be taught, at least by his tenth year, to pray for guidance in his choice of vocation. The choice may not be finally made until many years later, but it should be considered early. This consideration need not be presented to the child in so many words, but he should always know and feel that there are three states of life from which he must freely choose.

Nature of a Call

Vocation, often named a "calling," should not be explained to the child as an inner voice which clearly indicates God's Will. Rather, it shows itself by inclination, circumstances, ability, and, in religious or priestly vocation, by the acceptance or rejection of religious or ecclesiastical superiors.

Parents should teach these facts many times in word, but even more often by example. It should be the expressed desire of every family that God grant the grace of a religious or priestly vocation to one of the children. *Without exerting personal pressure of any kind,* mother and father should speak of the happiness it would give them if God granted this grace. They should always be reverent, admiring and devoted toward priests and nuns, who, with all their human faults, are God's special servants.

Toward those who live virginal lives in the world, parents should show admiration rather than pity. A girl or boy who remains unmarried to care for a family which has lost father or mother, should be respected and honored. A nurse, teacher or social worker, or anyone who consecrates a virginal life to real service of God and men, demands reverence and respect, not commiseration, or worse, cynical humor.

The sacredness of marriage should be continually expressed before the children, even though one or the other has clearly indicated a call to the virginal life. After all, religious and priests do not and should not despise marriage. It is a wholesome and good state which they have "traded in" for something better. A mature outlook on marriage is necessary for everyone. Marriage is noble! Teach your children by word and example that you married for love of each other and of children. Show reverence and love for each other, respect and esteem to other parents. Show that you consider your sacrifices worthwhile. As a means of teaching the sacredness of marriage, we suggest that you take the children to Wedding Masses and explain their beauty and deep meaning.

Your children are romantic. It is well, indeed, to show them the romance of all three states in life. Do not hide the difficulties of any state, but point out its value compared to the price that is paid. Hundreds of ways will suggest themselves to you. Storytelling from the Lives of the Saints (married saints, too!) will provide many such opportunities.

QUESTIONS AND DISCUSSION AIDS

1. Should sex education be separated from general education? Why not? Do you give a special education in honesty, truthfulness? Should the divisions of sex education be separated in teaching? Can you teach the religious first, the moral second, etc.?

2. A watch is made by a watchmaker to keep time. Who made man and for what purpose? How does man accomplish that purpose? What happens to a watch when it no longer keeps time? What happens to a man when he comes to the end of his life without reaching his goal?

3. What is a state of life? How many states are there? Which is the best? Why? Are the others evil? Which is the really right one for you? Discuss your reasons thoroughly.

4. Does a state in life have anything to do with sex education? Could you ever build a valid code of sexual morals without reference to God, and to state in life?

5. What are God's purposes for marriage? Is the order of purposes important? Why?

6. Is it not true that some parents have a few children for merely selfish reasons? What is the ideal of Christian parents?

   Discuss this verbatim report of a radio question addressed by one child to a panel of other children:[6]

   Questioner: "I want a dog but my mother won't let me have one."

   Answer: "You don't use the right strategy. Ask her for a baby brother—then I'm sure she'll settle for a dog."

7. Is a vocation an inner voice? What is it? How is it made known?

8. Do you give good example of respect toward all three callings? Is "old maid" frequent in your vocabulary? Can it be rightly applied to the unmarried by choice? Is virginity valuable in itself? Explain.

9. Do you really believe marriage is a career? Why is it a holy state? Do you ever indicate how happy you would be to see one of your children a priest or a nun? Would you be happy?

10. How would you use the beauty of a Wedding Mass to explain the nobility of marriage?

---

6. "Little Miffed Moppets," *Reader's Digest,* September, 1949, p. 47. Quoted with permission of the publisher.

Chapter VI

Religious Content of Catholic Sex Education: II

(THE CHALLENGE TO PURITY; MEANS TO ATTAIN IT)

REVERENCE FOR THE BODY

When once the meaning of vocation is known, the value of the body will become clear. The whole body is holy and sacred because God made it, because it is a cell of the Body of Christ, and a dwelling place of the Holy Spirit.

Modesty can easily be taught with the following religious background. After all, we clothe all the things we reverence. We cover the Tabernacle and the Ciborium with a veil. A priest brings the consecrated Chalice to the altar concealed under a beautiful liturgical covering. His consecrated body is clothed with vestments. In the same way, and with similar sentiments, the body should always be decently, and as far as is reasonably possible, appropriately clothed. It is holy. Let young people be taught this. Their natural desire for self-adornment can be consecrated and ennobled by the idea of showing reverence for their body, with its generative powers.

The sexual powers, far from being the least worthy, are among the most wonderful. Even among the marvelous bodily functions, certainly that one is unique which helps bring a human person into existence.

Our English words for the sex organs are not very satisfactory. "Genitals" is a technical term. "Private parts" sounds like a "No Trespassing" sign; it is correct, but very negative. The best word is a Latin one, "verenda." It means "the parts worthy of reverence." Besides the notion of reverence, the word has a tone of "modesty," indicating that these parts should be covered, and also a note of quiet fear, since they may so easily trick one into sin. If ever you doubt your own or your child's attitude, ask yourself whether you consider sexual organs as "verenda": as good and holy, a sacred trust from God to be used according to His laws.

Though sexual acts are beautiful and holy in marriage, they are shameful and vicious outside it. Just as it would be blasphemous and sacrilegious for a young man to pretend to say Mass or hear Confessions before his Ordination, so it is unholy for a young man to use his body before marriage as a married person does. Does this sound farfetched? Read St. Paul's condemnation of impurity as an *injustice,* a *sacrilege* and a *profanation* (*1 Cor.* 6:13-20):

> Now the body is not for immorality, but for the Lord, and the Lord for the body. . . .
> Do you not know that your bodies are members of Christ?
> Shall I then take the members of Christ and make them members of a harlot?
> By no means!
> Or do you not know that he who cleaves to a harlot, becomes one body with her? "For the two," it [Scripture] says, "shall be one flesh."
> But he who cleaves to the Lord is one spirit with Him. Flee immorality.
> Every [other] sin that a man commits is outside the body, but the immoral man sins against his own body.
> Or do you not know that your members are the temple of the Holy Spirit, who is in you, whom

you have from God, and that you are not your own?

For you have been bought at a great price.

Glorify God and bear Him in your body.

These words are startlingly strong, but they state truths inspired by God Himself.

This same reverence should extend to the bodies of others, for the following reasons:

First, they too are (at least possible) members of the Mystical Body of Christ and temples of the Holy Spirit.

Second, St. Thomas notes that any love for an external thing is selfish. A man, for example, who loves only food, is selfish. He wishes his own pleasure and nothing else. Therefore, if a man or woman desires a body, which is an external thing, and has no regard for the soul, his or her love is selfish. Since love is between persons, and persons are made of both soul and body, real love can never consider the body alone.

Finally, true love demands such reverence, for love demands that a man or woman do everything that is good for the beloved. To real love, death and torment mean nothing so long as the beloved one is benefited. Now, though it is true that sexual acts are the highest physical expression of love when used in marriage, nevertheless, when they occur outside of marriage such acts are really acts of hatred because the one who suggests them is really willing to see his beloved punished in Hell.

ESTEEM FOR PURITY

Once we understand all these facts, we cannot help loving chastity. It is a glorious virtue, a lily among thorns, which can be won only by hard work. It is a positive virtue, as is clear in the lives of Our Lady and Our Lord. Some moderns have the idea that purity is a weak, effeminate thing, and that lust alone is virile! (Notice the movie advertisements: "lusty," "sparkling," etc.) No, impurity is the weak, cowardly thing, that slinks off into a dark corner to enjoy its forbidden fruits. Let Chesterton show us how we should answer those who think purity is weak and sissified:

VIRTUE

I am sorry, old dear, if I hurt you,
No doubt it is all very nice,
With the lilies and languors of virtue
And the raptures and roses of vice.
But the notion impels me to anger
That vice is all rapture for me,
And if you think virtue is languor
JUST TRY IT AND SEE![1]

Natural Reasons for Purity

There are many good natural reasons for purity, but they are very weak compared to the vision of vocation and the holiness of the body, which we have shown you. Nevertheless, natural reasons are good reasons, and should be given along with the more religious instruction. Premarital chastity is very helpful toward a happy marriage, even on the most natural level.[2] The joys of parenthood, the realization of one's duty to humanity, perfect expression of married love, and a hundred other considerations demand chastity both before and during marriage. Most of these natural considerations will be dealt with in the chapters on emotion and psychology.

---

1. Ward, Maisie, *Gilbert Keith Chesterton* (Sheed and Ward, New York, 1943), p. 613. Quoted with permission of the copyright owner.
2. One has only to glance through the book, *Sexual Disorders*, by Dr. Max Huhner (F. H. Davis, Philadelphia, 1941), to be convinced of this. Cf. also, Bertocci, Peter A., *The Human Venture in Love, Sex and Marriage* (Association Press, New York, 1951).

ORIGINAL SIN

All this discussion about the religious and natural concept of sex and marriage—all these reasons, both positive and negative—would be sufficient to insure chastity in our youth, *if* (and it is a big IF) *there were no original sin!* Chesterton remarks that any man willing to see must perceive that there is a taint of some kind in human nature. Man, with all his ideals, hopes and plans, which are good and noble, frequently acts contrary to his own clear idea of what is right and wrong. Bishop Fulton J. Sheen has declared that the realization of the fact of original sin is more necessary today than the realization of any other doctrine. He has reason to say this. In one questionnaire, only 67 percent of Protestant ministers and 13 percent of students for the Protestant ministry held the doctrine of original sin! (Incidentally, only 9 percent of the students believed in a devil.)

What Is It?

In Paradise, Adam and Eve did not obey God's command. Because of their sin they lost sanctifying grace, the right to Heaven, and their special gifts; they became subject to death, to suffering, to ignorance, and to a *strong inclination to evil.* On account of Adam's sin, we, his descendants, come into the world deprived of sanctifying grace, and inherit all his punishments. This sin in us is called original sin.

The most disconcerting of its effects is an inborn contrariness in us. We, who are made for God, tend away from Him. We, who are made to be good and virtuous, tend away from the very good we should pursue. Original sin in us has left our will toward true moral good weakened, and our inclinations disordered, rebellious and violent. We find it hard to keep the simplest resolution for a single day. We find that if we do not strenuously fix our aim on God and on virtuous acts, and beg His aid to achieve them, we are soon full of shameful evil. St. Paul has put it exactly (*Rom.* 7:22-23, 15):

> For I am delighted with the law of God according to the inner man,
> But I see another law in my members, warring against the law of my mind and making me a prisoner to the law of sin that is in my members.
> . . . it is not what I wish that I do, but what I hate, that I do.

Who has not experienced this warring of members which St. Paul describes? Yet how many of us attempt to live without taking this natural flaw into account!

Natural Means

The presence of this flaw is the reason why the Church and the Popes are so strong in condemning merely natural means for preserving chastity. However good the natural methods, they are *not strong enough* to combat humanity's inborn weakness. As Pius XI says, in the encyclical *On the Christian Education of Youth:*

> . . . Every form of pedagogic *naturalism* which in any way *excludes* or *weakens* supernatural Christian formation in the teaching of youth, is false.[3]

The realization of the impact of original sin is also the reason why we, as Catholics, must oppose so much of the "sex education" that is proposed for public schools. Such sex information is given on the assumption that human nature is completely good without any help from God, and that instruction or information can never be harmful. Some educators believe that once young people know all about the physiology and the emotional content of sexual relations, and also the danger of venereal disease, they will live chaste lives. Experience

---

3. Natural helps which do not exclude the supernatural are not, of course, condemned.

proves over and over again that this simply is not true.[4] The most recent non-Catholic thinkers on the problem have begun to abandon such ideas and now support a broader idea of "sex education" which is not quite so far from our Catholic one.[5]

Original Sin and Sex

More people are betrayed into sins by ignorance of their weak human nature than by any other single factor. They feel confident, strong, captains of their fate. They dally with all sorts of temptations, relying on their natural powers alone to keep them from lying, theft and lust. They refuse to admit that their own worst enemy is within. When they read of fantastic evils, the sadistic cruelties of the recent war, and the staggering sex crimes of our day, they label the criminals as "insane." They are fools! Though crimes of this nature have been committed by the insane, *most crimes are committed by normal people who have deliberately placed themselves in a series of situations in which their unfortified wills succumb.* We all have within us the seeds of every kind of sin, and only the most realistic precautions can save us. The sexual passions are the most difficult tendencies to control, and original sin creates more havoc in that realm than in any other. This fact demands that we study and adopt correct attitudes toward sexual sin.

Parents' Attitudes

Parents must realize the struggle that their children face through late childhood and adolescence. They must not ignore, nor must they be horrified by, the fact that their children can be tempted or can sin. When their

---

4. Cf. "Psychologic Aspects of Sex Education," in the U. S. Armed Forces Medical Journal, Supplement, July-August, 1951
5. Cf. Gruenberg, Benjamin C., *How Can We Teach about Sex?*, Public Affairs Pamphlet No. 122, New York, Public Affairs Committee, Inc., 1946.

children are maturing sexually, parents should be sympathetic and helpful. They should recall their own difficulties and prepare themselves to help their children. Parents should not show horror or fly into a rage if a child falls or even develops a habit of sin. They must try to imitate our Lord, who condemned the *sin* but helped the *sinner.* These statements take it for granted that the child will come to you for help. This in turn presupposes that the child has confidence in you. If these things are not true in your case, there is little you can do but pray and show yourself willing to aid. You can and must correct external acts, but a child will probably resent any intrusion into his internal affairs.

Children's Attitudes

Children must be taught that goodness will not come without effort. As with so many things, they learn this more easily from experience than from words. The child must learn self-control in all things, with gradual application to purity and modesty as needed. Therefore, sensible parents will repress temper tantrums, selfishness, excessive softness and comfort, choice of only the pleasing foods, and so on. The child will thus learn that he may not do, say, read and see whatever he wishes in life. A child should also learn that not all duties in life are agreeable and pleasant, yet that by the "hard work" of duty he obtains worthwhile things. Purity is one of these virtues most worthwhile. It is important also that moderation be taught in all things that give pleasure, especially bodily pleasure. There is a weighty reason behind such moderation. Man is not on earth for pleasure, but pleasure is given him to smooth out the road a little. If pleasure is made the purpose of life, no one can be chaste. If pleasure is the goal of life, no one will reach Heaven.

Discipline and Mortification

Well-ordered home life demands discipline in many matters. Such home discipline should prepare the way for the practice of chastity, which also demands discipline particularly in the realm of thought and imagination. This mental discipline is taught better by *direction* than by *repression*. If a child is expected to apply himself diligently to his studies without daydreaming; to perform duties suitable to his age; to stick to a job until it is finished—he will learn this necessary discipline of thought and imagination.

Mortification should also be a commonplace in the Catholic home. Friday abstinence, little Lenten mortifications, and tiny voluntary sacrifices offered to God, develop a self-control in the child which will carry over for life. When St. Thérèse, the Little Flower of Jesus, was but five years old, she carried a tiny "counting rosary" to number her mortifications during the day. Though they may well omit her method of counting, children certainly need her kind of sensible and mild mortification.

Motive—Love of God

A child should be given all possible good motives for sacrifice, mortification and self-control. He or she should learn self-control in order to become manly or womanly, to please mother or father, to be generous to others, to show love for others, to win friends, etc. *The chief motive, however, should always be love of God.* Sacrifice for love of God is the greatest experience in a human life and this motive is surprisingly strong in even the tiniest tot. To foster and feed it, teach your children the part God has played in their existence, redemption, and hope of Heaven. Kindle love in their hearts for the Infant in the manger, for the Boy Jesus in Nazareth, for the weary Teacher who was not too busy to cure little children or to play with and caress them. Stir their ardor for a Hero who did not shrink from pouring out His blood as satisfaction for their sins. Challenge them to follow a Leader who has shown them the way to Heaven. With a burning and personal love for Jesus Christ as He is made real to them in all the details of His life and Passion, children will not find it so difficult to be mortified and self-controlled. Indeed, once inflamed by this love, they may easily outdistance their parents.

PRAYER AND THE SACRAMENTS

Prayer

Since evil tendencies are so strong within us, everyone should be accustomed to pray for help in every temptation. Training children in prayer is discussed in many booklets on education in the home. Here we shall merely point out the connection of prayer and chastity. Anyone who has faced difficulties in regard to purity will testify that daily prayer has helped tremendously. Three "Hail Marys" for purity, on rising and before going to bed, are very powerful. Little aspirations in times of temptation are lifesavers. Such a prayer in times of temptation, if only the utterance of the names of Jesus and Mary, has a double effect: it shows clearly that one is not consenting to the disturbing temptation, and it draws down God's grace to help combat the evil suggestion.

Our Lady

Devotion to the Blessed Virgin as our Model of Purity should flourish in every home. Thousands of men and women, both saints and ordinary folk, testify to the power of her name in temptations against purity. If you want your children to be chaste through life, do not omit this important family devotion to Our Lady. In matters of sex information, it is particularly -

helpful to connect the "facts of life" to events in our Blessed Mother's life; for example, the idea of pregnancy and the period of gestation can be shown by pointing out the nine months between March 25, the Annunciation, and December 25, Christmas; or between December 8, the Immaculate Conception, and September 8, the birthday of Our Lady. Such an example for the facts of life gives a religious and emotional setting to the information which will help prevent undesirable effects on the child.

The Sacraments—Penance and Holy Communion

Though all the Sacraments give the graces needed for our daily lives, Penance and Holy Eucharist give the most frequently accessible support to chastity. All Catholics should cling to the regular and frequent reception of these two Sacraments. To this end children should acquire the habit of weekly Confession, and weekly or even daily Holy Communion, since the success of their struggle for chastity depends largely on the early acquisition of this holy practice. Young people will walk safely through the pitfalls of modern temptation if they keep close to these sources of grace. Besides all this, should a child contract a habit of impurity, weekly Confession and Communion is a "must" if that habit is to be broken.

The Sacraments may well be approached as a family affair, since the parents' example is everything in this matter. If children are urged to go to Confession and Holy Communion, to pray, and to make sacrifices, while their parents do none of these things, they will unconsciously conclude that all this is "kid stuff," to be discarded as soon as they reach maturity. Let the mother take the younger children to Confession in the afternoon, and the father go with the adolescents in the evening. Why not a family Communion from time to time? Why not a family Communion breakfast for the family feasts, anniversaries and birthdays or on the

Sundays following them? In all this, let the sentiment be natural, unaffected; children are the first to notice insincerity in parents.

A Caution

Some cautions in connection with Confession and Communion should be laid down, however. *First, make sure that everyone is free to go or not! Again, never act suspicious if the child spends some time in the confessional. Lastly, never question him about what he said there.* If the child wishes to go to Confession alone, by all means let him! He may wish to spend some time in the confessional for a good reason, or no serious reason at all, but he should be free. Similarly, there should be no scolding if the child does not go to Communion on a certain day. He may even be instructed that he may deliberately break his fast to avoid going to Communion with the rest, if he feels that he should not go. If a child should break his fast, do not be suspicious. It may have been accidental, or it may have been deliberate in order to prevent a "bad" Communion. In either case there is no call to probe for the child's reason. Your reaction to the information given shortly before Mass, "Mother, I ate something when I was downstairs a few minutes ago!"[6] should be: "Too bad, dear—you can't go to Communion today. You can go some other time." Briefly then, though the habit of frequent approach to the Sacraments should be formed by family custom, no personal pressure of any kind should be brought to bear. Family members should be *expected* to be virtuous and regular at the sacraments, but they should not be *forced,* on any given occasion, to approach the confessional, or receive Communion. Any fear of outside pressure or interference might lead them to

---

6. The Church's law of fasting before Holy Communion now requires us to fast three hours from food and alcoholic drinks and one hour from non-alcoholic drinks before Communion. The drinking of water is permitted at any time before Communion. Note: The Church's law now requires only a one-hour fast from food and liquids— except for water, which is permitted at any time before Communion.—*Editor,* 1993.

approach these Sacraments sacrilegiously—a sad effect of misguided zeal.

It is well to *advise* a child to choose a regular confessor, particularly if there is question of deciding a religious vocation, of curing scrupulosity, or of correcting a sinful habit. On the other hand, it is also a good idea to explain the wisdom of approaching a strange confessor whenever shame might prevent complete candor with a confessor the child knows. Here, as in the occasions described above, a child's freedom is paramount.

Confirmation

The value of several other Sacraments should be pointed up in connection with Christian chastity. Matrimony and Holy Orders give graces needed to preserve the chastity of those states in life, and all who receive them have a right to the graces attached to them. There is no room for discussion of these Sacraments here. Confirmation, however, demands more attention.

This is the Sacrament of Christian maturity, of Christian strength and fortitude. It is the Sacrament that gives us the courage to confess our Faith in word and in deed. Whenever an appeal is made to the virility of our young men and the womanliness of our young women, emphasis should be placed on this Sacrament, and particularly when modern customs attack purity or modesty. It is extremely difficult for young people to swim against the stream. Yet, when it comes to the question of "everybody does it" in dating, dress, etc., Catholics simply must be *different* if such customs are sinful or dangerous. Confirmation is the Sacrament designed by Christ to enable Catholics *to be different* in such cases. The graces of Confirmation must be used, and strengthened by prayer.

Soldiers of Christ are inducted by the Sacrament of Confirmation. They even may be said to have a special uniform—the uniform of modesty and purity of morals.

QUESTIONS AND DISCUSSION AIDS

1. Why is the body, all of it, holy? How can you engender reverence for it in children? Should we not reverence the bodies of others also? Have you ever read anything stronger than St. Paul's condemnation of impurity?

2. Are our Hollywood actors and actresses helping this reverence by their glorification of the body?

3. We know you will not be able to use the Latin word "verenda," but isn't it a good test for proper attitudes? Can you think of or invent a similar English one? How would you teach this reverence by referring to clothing?

4. Discuss methods of teaching love for purity in a positive way. Is purity a virile thing? Or is it more virile to be "lusty" in the sense of "full of lust"? Are the generative functions a sacred, challenging trust?

5. What is original sin? What has it to do with education to chastity? What is wrong with merely natural reasons as a defense against impurity? As an argument against sex education in public schools, a mother once said: "You cannot handle the topic in school without morality; morality is impossible without religion; you are forbidden to consider religion in the public schools. Therefore, I submit that you may not give public sex instruction." Is there any weak link in this chain of reasoning?

6. Do you think ignorance of the flaw in our nature is the cause of many a downfall? Is it not true that we are all capable of the most revolting crimes if we let down our defenses?

7. If children realize this flaw, should it make them cautious of the snares to purity in life? Jerry, a boy of 16, sat alone till the wee hours of the morning with Anna, a girl the same age. Granting no evil intention in either of them, should their knowledge of original sin have prohibited this?

8. What is the best motive for virtuous acts? Does this preclude lesser motives?

9. What are the chief means of obtaining supernatural help?

From your own experience, did these means help you? Why should there be a great deal of freedom in approaching the Sacraments? Discuss ways and means of making religious helps a part of family living.

10. What are some good aspirations for times of temptation against chastity? What is the double advantage of quick prayer in times of stress?

11. Are your children encouraged to little private mortifications? Do you lead the way in this? Discuss some possible opportunities of mortification—at table, in family games, in sharing toys, in not choosing the best of everything, in giving in to others, etc. Are you honestly convinced of the value of mortification?

12. Why do we say that Holy Communion from early years gives us our only hope for the purity of youth? Have there ever been worse snares to purity than today?

13. After our brief exposition, have you learned a new respect for the Sacraments of Confirmation and Matrimony? Discuss your reactions together.

Chapter VII

Moral Content of
Catholic Sex Education: I

(CHASTITY—PRINCIPLES I AND II)

Catholics who have had any religious training at all usually know a great deal about ethics or morals. They know what is right or wrong, and the conditions in which it is right and wrong. For example, Catholics well know that stealing is wrong. They know, however, that the amount taken and the wealth or poverty of the person from whom it is taken, changes the degree of guilt; they know, too, that to take food if one is actually starving, is not sinful at all. Practicing Catholics know about the obligations of Mass on Sunday, of abstinence on Friday, and the conditions under which these obligations do *not* bind. And so on with many other things.

However, a large number of Catholics are very hazy about the principles of sex morality both in and out of marriage. It is our contention that *all* Catholics should know these principles and at least the general application of them to their own lives. To know this much will not make you a moral theologian, for there will still be many cases that require the judgment of a skilled confessor. When you study the principles set down here, be assured that you can learn them and apply them. They are no more difficult than any of the other moral principles by which you guide your daily lives.

CHILDREN AND SEXUAL MORALITY

The child, and particularly the adolescent, should gradually learn the principles of right and wrong in sexual matters. Children are growing to adult life, and they must be trained little by little to meet difficulties, to judge and act *for themselves.* They cannot, and if they could, they should not, run to Mother and Dad in every moral problem they will encounter. It is nothing short of criminal to *be* the conscience of a child throughout his whole growing life. He must eventually face his fate alone. When the time comes, he should be able to do so. Any training (or lack of it) which sends a child out into the temptations of our modern world without ability to judge for himself, is responsible either for many sexual sins, or for a neurotic, scrupulous mind unfit for a life of decision. A child must be weaned in all spheres so that he may gradually become independent. This is true for moral living as well as for physical and emotional living.

Scrupulosity

Some people think that scrupulosity is a sign of virtue. If by scrupulosity were meant attention to the elimination of venial sins and even of the slightest deliberate faults, this would be true. But scrupulosity does not mean that. Scrupulosity is a state in which a person is disturbed about sin when there is *no* fault at all, or in which he is no longer able to judge what is serious, what is light, or what is not sinful in any degree. He is forever worrying about being in the state of grace, about whether *all* his sins were told in Confession, etc. *Such an unbalanced attitude is a defect, not a virtue.* It may indicate unruly pride; at the very least it usually means that the individual is too self-centered. A woman is an excellent housekeeper if she attends carefully to order and cleanliness in the home. If, however, she considers a footmark equivalent to a cyclone of disorder; if she continually dusts the same piece of furniture to "make sure" it is dusted; if she cannot be certain that she has cleaned the room properly and insists on going over it again and again—then she is a fair example of the way a scrupulous person torments himself in moral matters.

In the realm of purity, attention to venial sin or to dangerous occasions, is a healthy sign of virtue. But if one thinks that slight faults are serious; if one can never make up one's mind whether an act is mortal or venial or neither; if one is continually worrying about whether he committed a sin or not; if he goes over and over the same matter and never really reaches a conclusion; or if he concludes that a doubtful action is a mortal sin "just to be safe"—then he is scrupulous. Such scrupulosity (except in the rare case where it is allowed by God as a trial) is unhealthy and does positive harm to one's spiritual life.

God does not demand absolute certainty in our acts. He demands only that we give the same reasonable care to the morality of our acts that we give to any other important matter. If we act on a prudent judgment, if we confess our sins as far as we honestly can, we have fulfilled His law. A case of scrupulosity demands a skilled confessor who will create in the penitent an ability (at least finally) to make a decision about an act and to follow it out without worrying and seesawing from yes to no. The lack of this ability in some people is one reason why we insist on your knowing the moral principles. They will enable you to reach decisions and act!

Will They Understand?

Many people may object that a child will not understand these moral principles. We admit that he will not *fully* understand them, for all the possibilities of application cannot, and indeed, should not, be made. Yet, children do not fully understand other things they are taught. They learn the catechism without full understanding, and gradually "fill in" as they grow older. They should learn these moral principles and their application in the same way.

When Should They Learn Them?

Your children should learn these principles as they need them. This means that general principles of modesty should be known in early years, between 6 and 10. By the time that sexual pleasure is at hand, they should know *all* the principles. This means that when the "facts of life" are taught, the moral principles must also be taught. Certainly in our modern times, every boy and girl 14 years of age should know these principles and be able to apply them to the ordinary dangers they meet.

GENERAL CONDITIONS FOR SERIOUS SIN

A person commits a serious, or mortal, sin only when he 1) breaks a moral law in a serious matter, 2) does so knowingly and consciously, and 3) chooses the action with full and free consent of his will. Therefore, if he doesn't realize the serious nature of what he is doing, if he is not free, or if he does not really give consent with his will, the action is at most venially sinful. For example, if John, aged 3, handles his genitals, he commits no sin because he can have no idea such an action could be wrong. May, aged 10, who accidentally discovers masturbation, probably commits no sin the first time for the same reason. Both must be corrected, however. John should be corrected lightly with the same emphasis given to a correction for sucking his thumb. Someone must speak seriously to May and tell her that she did an act which was sinful, even though she did not realize it and was not guilty at the time. Such correction is necessary because a habit of this sort is easily formed, and a tremendous struggle may be needed to break it.

Delight and Pleasure

Pleasure is something that resides in the body. It is there, for the most part, without our desiring it. For example, perfume smells pleasant whether we wish it to do so or not. Velvet or fur feels agreeable to the touch whether we consent to the feeling or not. In these cases, however, we can usually get away from the source of the pleasure if we so will. This is not always true of venereal, or sexual, pleasure. At times, it comes against one's will. But it must not be *delighted in* with the will; that is, it must not be wished, wanted, caused, approved, or deliberately enjoyed outside of marriage. This is very important. At times, sexual pleasure, particularly in the male, arises from no apparent cause. At other times, when there is a cause, the individual has a lawful reason for continuing the actions which have incidentally brought about this pleasure. *Sin lies in willful consent or deliberate delight, not necessarily in the mere experience of bodily pleasure.*

MORAL PRINCIPLES FOR THE UNMARRIED

With these preliminaries out of the way, let us consider the moral principles for *all who are not married.* There are four such principles and they cover every possible case, though they may be difficult to apply to some particular case without the help of a confessor. Two principles concern impurity and two concern immodesty. Those concerning impurity will be treated in this chapter, those concerning immodesty will be studied in the following one.

1. *To bring about deliberately even the slightest venereal pleasure, alone or with someone else, or to delight in it with the will if it is accidentally aroused, is always a mortal sin.* If you do not like this phrasing, here is the same principle in simpler language, though it is not so complete: *It is a mortal sin to seek, to cause, or to take willful*

delight in sexual pleasure (or venereal pleasure, or sexual excitement), whether such pleasure is complete or incomplete.

Notice that this principle holds for *all* sins of impurity, whether committed alone or with another of either sex. It places responsibility on the individual. As soon as he experiences this impure pleasure, which should not be confused with any other bodily feeling, he must *refuse consent*. This is best done by the recitation of a prayer.

What is venereal or sexual pleasure? It is that physical or bodily pleasure which accompanies the excitation of the sexual organs. The pleasure is *in* those organs. In the male it begins with a stiffening of the penis (called erection) and is completed by a series of nervous impulses (called orgasm) with, after puberty, the ejaculation of semen. In the female this pleasure is more diffused for it begins with a stiffening or swelling of the breasts and genital regions, together with a slight vaginal discharge. It is completed by a keen pleasurable commotion in the genital region (called orgasm or "satisfaction") which relieves the tension of passion and is accompanied by a greater flow of vaginal fluid. Orgasm alone is considered *complete pleasure,* while all strictly sexual pleasure short of orgasm is considered *incomplete pleasure.* For the unmarried, both complete and incomplete pleasure are mortal sins if the will approves, though the first is of a more serious kind than the second, and each must be confessed as a different kind of sin.

Venereal pleasure must be distinguished, however, from other bodily feelings which are not in themselves sinful. The thrill of a first kiss in adolescence, the intense excitement that comes with a wild roller-coaster ride, the feeling of contentment that lovers experience in each other's company, the tightening in the abdomen when fear is present, the emotion of shame at being caught in some disgrace, the feeling of a blush, are not venereal feelings. We mention this because many youngsters, particularly boys, experience their first sexual awakening in connection with some other emotion.[1] Some adolescents have mistaken a wild *fear* at some vivid, immodest picture or imagination for sexual pleasure! If they come to you, carefully separate the two, so that no habits of association will be formed. Otherwise, it is possible that an individual may come to be sexually excited whenever he has any one of these other physical feelings.

Obviously, all this should not be taught the child at an early age. There is the danger that he might experiment to find out what this pleasure is. Yet, once the child has reached the age of puberty, he or she may begin to experience these stings of the flesh, and must be taught to apply this principle. At first it will be enough to say: "Being impure is a serious sin." Later, you can add: "Deliberately to enjoy sexual pleasure is a serious sin." If they must know what sexual pleasure is, tell them it is the pleasure that arises in the generative organs (or private parts, or whatever term you wish to use). Or it may be defined as the peculiar sensation or feeling which comes when the sex organs are seriously excited.

Application

Let us apply the first principle to some concrete cases.

1. A boy finds that in sliding down a bannister, or in riding a bicycle, he becomes sexually excited. He rejects the pleasure and immediately starts on a ball game. He has not sinned, for he has not willed or consented to the pleasure that accidentally arose. (If he has said a brief prayer, he is doubly certain. One cannot really pray and sin mortally at the same time.)

2. A girl indulges in romantic daydreams in order to arouse a slight sexual thrill. She sins mortally, be-

---

1. Cf. Ramsey, Glenn V., "The Sexual Development of Boys," in the *American Journal of Psychology*, April, 1943, pp. 222-223, 232.

cause the pleasure is deliberately sought. If she starts to daydream without evil intention, then finds herself becoming excited and at once rejects the pleasure, she has not sinned, she has only been tempted. (Not sufficient reflection or consent.)

3. A boy and girl on a date seek all the sexual thrills they can obtain without "going the limit." They both sin mortally, even though one of them, as a matter of fact, experienced no pleasure at all! Their intention was bad. If the pleasure of either was complete, that fact must be confessed, since complete pleasure or "satisfaction" is a different kind of sin than incomplete lust.

4. A boy awakens at night from a "sexy" dream accompanied by a seminal emission. He immediately says a prayer, rolls over, and goes to sleep. He has not sinned. If he consents while fully awake, he sins seriously. But if he is only half awake, even though he seems to consent, or even stimulates it by actions, his sin is at most venial; for though the matter is serious, his consent and deliberation were vague and incomplete.

This principle must not be put before the child in all its possible applications; remember what we have said about *ignorance of evil.* There is no reason, however, why the boy of 12 and the girl a year younger (or children still younger, if circumstances require it) should not memorize this principle with the others still to be discussed in one of its forms. Application should come as needed. The first application will probably come at the first seminal emission or menstruation.[2] Adolescents, especially on their first dates, will need other applications; company-keepers will need more. Those who go out to work or into special dangers will need still further applications. Do not try to anticipate all

---

2. Menstruation has no direct connection with sexual pleasure for menstruation and sexual pleasure may take place apart from each other. The appearance of menstruation, however, is usually a good indication that sexual pleasure is possible to a girl. It may only appear later, but the lesson should be learned at this time if it has not already been learned, or before this if the child has stumbled upon self-stimulation (self-abuse, or masturbation).

possibilities. The advantage of this principle lies in the fact that all sins of lust, even perversions of which I could wish my readers were ignorant, will be guarded against. The principle is a yardstick which fits every case. Should the individual meet a temptation of an unusual sort, he will be prepared to apply this principle and make a proper decision.

CAUTION: To this instruction *always add* that sex pleasure is sacred and normal in marriage and that temptations, imaginings, and spontaneous sex arousal are not abnormal in growing young people. They are a sign of approaching maturity. Make clear that *all* young people face this problem. To the boy, explain the purpose of nocturnal pollutions (cf. Chapter XI of this book). This occurrence is natural and normal to all males. It need not occasion the faintest worry to the young man who wills to remain pure (cf. *ibid.,* pp. 108-110, on emotion in connection with these facts).

2. Desires and Thoughts: *Deliberately to desire or wish forbidden sexual pleasure is a mortal sin, even though no bodily pleasure arises.*

To think with willful approval or mental satisfaction of impurity of any kind is a mortal sin even though no physical pleasure arises.

These two principles, on Desire and Thought, may be phrased together in simpler fashion: *Wanting to perform an impure action, or thinking with approval of anyone being impure, is a mortal sin.*

Clearly, desiring an evil is a sin of the same kind as the evil desired, for God demands that we love His order as well as keep it. If we were to desire something against His plan, we would show that we do not love His Will for us, and we would immediately open ourselves to the next step—that of violating it in action. In reference to chastity, Our Lord makes this limpidly clear: "I say to you that anyone who so much as looks with lust at a woman has already committed adultery with her in his heart" (*Matt.* 5:28).

The sin of "bad" or impure thoughts consists in taking delight with the will in the imagination or thought of sinful actions, whether these actions are one's own or another's. This does not mean that one may not think of impurity in general or in particular, granted that the will does not approve it. If all thoughts of impurity were sinful, no one could read this book, or learn sexual facts, or listen to warnings from the pulpit, or even read an examination of conscience! For a thought to be strictly *impure* it must be a deliberate picturing of someone (most frequently, of course, the picturer will involve himself) enjoying forbidden sex pleasure, with the will definitely approving the action with its forbidden element. Notice, however, that many thoughts which might not be "bad" thoughts in this strict sense (that is, there is no approval of the impurity) can easily be immodest thoughts (that is, of such a nature as to stimulate sexual passion). These will be considered in the next chapter.

Most thoughts and desires have more the nature of temptation than of sin; for no matter how long a vivid imagination lasts, it is not sinful until approved by the will. There is, however, a certain natural inclination to such thoughts. When an impure idea or desire arises unbidden, there is a first, almost compelling impulse toward it. After all, sexual pleasure is a natural good in itself, and it is attractive. *This first impulse is not sinful.* It is only when one's will gives the go-ahead signal that the desire or thought becomes sinful.

Applying this principle on desire and thought, we give three cases:

1. A young man deliberately desires to sin with a young woman, though he makes no effort to do so for fear of social consequences. He sins mortally.

2. A young woman daydreams with approving delight of venereal pleasure with a man. She does not go so far as desiring actually to accomplish it, nor does she take any positive action to cause personal plea-

sure. She nevertheless sins mortally.

3. A young man realizes the pleasures of married life. He desires some day to enjoy them in marriage. He commits no sin of impurity in such a thought, because what he desires in marriage is lawful there, though his thought might be immodest. When such a thought would be sinfully immodest will be explained in the next chapter.

QUESTIONS AND DISCUSSION AIDS

1. Is it right to decide all moral questions for a child? When should children learn the moral principles concerning chastity and modesty? Do you think it a good idea to make them memorize these even without understanding?

2. What are the conditions for a serious sin? Propose some cases in explaining your answer.

3. Give some examples of "natural" scrupulosity. *(The individual who felt the key turn in the lock, yet worries about whether he locked the door; the woman who can't sleep because she fears she left the light on or the water running, even though she checked before going to bed; etc.)* Is scrupulosity ever spiritually beneficial? Does God demand that, before acting, we be as certain of the morality of our act as of our own existence? Is it possible to be scrupulous over sex education? *(I caused them to sin. I didn't. Etc., etc.)* Will this make it difficult to continue? What does common sense tell you of all these practical matters? *(After cautious consideration, act reasonably and leave the rest to God.)*

4. Solve this case: Jack, aged 16, observes in a postcard rack some pictures which are obscene or nearly obscene. He doesn't realize the fact, and walks by thinking of them. After a minute or two he says to himself, "Wait a minute, those things are immodest pictures!" Has he sinned so far, even granting the pictures were seriously stimulating? Why or why not?

5. What is the difference between delight (or joy) and pleasure? *(Delight or joy is in the will, pleasure is in the senses.)*

6. Define chastity (see Chapter I). Can you state the first moral principle of unmarried chastity in one of its two forms? (see p. 79). Define sexual or venereal pleasure (see three forms of definition on pp. 80 and 81). Discuss the cases on pp. 81-82, 84, and try to prepare other cases for solution. Consult a priest if you cannot solve them.

7. Give one form of the second principle on thought and desire. What is the important idea in an impure thought? *(Thinking with willing approval.)* Bring forward some applications of this moral principle.

8. Is desire for venereal pleasure always a serious sin? Give one case when it is not. *(Desire for it in marriage.)* Did you know previously that the first impulse toward something implying venereal pleasure is not in itself sinful? Will knowledge of this fact prevent worry?

Chapter VIII

Moral Content of Catholic Sex Education: II

(MODESTY—PRINCIPLES III AND IV)

IMMODESTY

The two principles in the preceding chapter refer to impurity in its strict sense; that is, to the *willing enjoyment* of unlawful sexual pleasure, in action, desire or thought. The principles explained in this chapter apply to immodesty; that is, they apply to those actions which, though indifferent in themselves, *may be causes* of illicit sexual pleasure in oneself or others. Such actions may be sinful in various degrees or not at all sinful; it depends on, first, the danger of consent to the consequent pleasure; second, the degree of connection with sexual pleasure; and third, the reason for performing such actions. Since these conditions vary with each person and with each action, the application of the principles concerning immodesty is difficult. Yet in spite of this difficulty, every person can and should have an understanding of the principles sufficient for his own personal needs in ordinary cases. Extraordinary cases should be referred to a confessor.

The Third Principle of sexual morality, then, considers actions which, though neither good nor bad in themselves, may arouse even unwanted sexual pleasure in oneself. The Fourth Principle considers similar actions which may arouse lust of any kind or even unwanted sexual pleasure in others.

3. *Granted that the danger of consent to any venereal pleasure which might be aroused, is remote*—Principle I—*any deliberate thought, imagination, reading, look, touch, or anything else which may arouse sexual feelings is a mortal or venial sin, or no sin at all, depending on the degree of sexual stirring such acts cause in proportion to the reason for acting.*

This principle is not so involved as it looks. Let us consider it phrase by phrase. Danger of consent must be remote; that is, an individual must know (usually from experience) that in certain thoughts, reading, etc., he rarely consents to any physical pleasure. If a person knows he *usually consents* to the sexual pleasure arising from a look, touch, etc., he must avoid it (Principle I). For him, it is a proximate occasion of sin, and such close dangers of sinful consent must be avoided. However, an occasional fall does not necessarily imply that a proximate occasion of sin is present.

Even though danger of consent is slight, *any action which of its nature leads to even unwilled sexual pleasure is sinful, if done without a good reason.* It is a *serious sin* if the action is closely connected with this pleasure and there is little or no reasonable motive for doing it; for example, intimate touches between adolescents. It is a *venial sin* if the action is only slightly connected with sex pleasure and there is hardly any reason for the action; for example, for a boy to look at the picture of an immodestly clad girl deliberately but without evil intention. It is *no sin at all* if the action is not ordinarily connected with such pleasure; for example, the boy who experiences the pleasure while riding a bicycle; or if there is a reason which outweighs the danger of such physical pleasure; for example, a doctor treating women. Therefore, two things must be checked in this principle of immodesty. First, the connection of the act in question with venereal pleasure.

Second, the reason for doing it. Naturally the closer the connection, the greater the reason needed if the action is to be blameless.

The Connection of the Act with Sex Pleasure

The connection of any act with sex pleasure depends, in turn, on two conditions: the *sensibility of the individual concerned,* and the *nature of the act.* Each individual gradually finds out what affects him, and must refrain accordingly. In cases where acts stimulate him which are not ordinarily connected with sex pleasure, for example, a boy riding a bicycle, a boy looking at another boy in a bathing suit, or a girl at another girl, etc., these should ordinarily be simply ignored.

The stimulating nature of different acts depends on what is done and to whom it is directed. An act directed to one of the opposite sex is usually more stimulating than the same act toward one's own sex. A passionate kiss is different from a brotherly kiss, and so on. Some acts are very stimulating because they are the ordinary preliminaries to the act of sexual mating. If one has no right to the marital act (that is, is not married), he has no right to the preliminaries. Such preliminaries are: passionate kisses and embraces, "heavy" petting, touching the private parts of the body, etc.[1]

Other acts are only slightly stimulating; for example, a light embrace or kiss. Granted that consent is not given to any accidental sex pleasure, these are *venial sins* if done without a good reason.

To give you some norms by which to judge, a series of acts is listed below. Those of the first group are considered seriously sinful for the ordinary person, if done

---

1. Many non-Catholic writers are now recognizing these facts, and urging young people to avoid such actions as being cheap and only imitations of true marital love. They argue that: 1) Heavy petting teases the emotions without satisfying them, thus making self-control more difficult; 2) Petting is properly a prelude to the marital act; 3) It is selfish since it is done for the thrill, not for love; 4) It breaks down reserve; 5) It cheapens personality; 6) Many half-experiences make the next temptation greater. Cf. Edson, *Love, Courtship and Marriage* (American Social Hygiene Association, New York, 1933).

without a justifying reason:

1. Deliberately looking at a person of the opposite sex entirely or almost nude. Looking at really obscene pictures or illustrations (unless very briefly).

2. Touching the private parts of the bodies of the same or opposite sex, deliberately and/or lingeringly.

3. Attending highly suggestive or indecent movies, plays, burlesque, etc.

4. Petting and kissing which are passionate or prolonged.

5. Suggestive or immoral dancing.

6. Holding obscene thoughts in the mind. Note the difference from *impure* thoughts, explained above (Principle II in preceding chapter).

7. Telling or listening to extremely immoral and suggestive stories.

The following actions are ordinarily venial sins unless justified by a sufficient reason:

1. Immodest looks at the opposite sex (for example, in a bathing attire) in a passing way or from curiosity or frivolity.

2. Embraces, kissing, "light" petting, indulged in for short periods or out of levity. (Ordinary kissing games belong here, as also many teen-age activities that cause parents and superiors a good deal of worry.)

3. Telling lightly suggestive stories or reading them.

4. Suggestive thoughts entertained for a brief time, listening to "dirty jokes" *for the humorous element,* etc.

The Reason

In determining what might be a good reason for these acts, it must be kept in mind that the reason must be proportionate to the effect. A doctor must do many things in his study and profession which may cause venereal pleasure. This is also true for nurses, educators, social workers, and many others. Again, a child must learn some sexual matters as he grows older, despite the fact that this knowledge may be stimulating. Moreover, recreational reading excuses the excitation that might arise from some of the pictures seen in the ordinary magazine, or the scenes described in ordinary stories or books. The most that can be laid down as a norm is this: acts of such a nature as to cause satisfaction or near-satisfaction demand a very serious reason to justify them. Acts which only slightly arouse the passions may be done for a lesser reason. Remember, however, that all this holds only IF THERE IS NO SERIOUS DANGER OF CONSENT; that is, deliberate delight in the venereal pleasure which might arise.

We shall put this in schema form to make it easy to remember:

1. Acts which of their nature may lead to sexual pleasure depend:
   a) on the excitability of the individual;
   b) on the stimulating nature of the act and the person to whom it is directed.

2. These acts, done *without* a good reason are:
   a) mortally sinful if they are of such a nature as to arouse complete or nearly complete pleasure;
   b) venially sinful if they are of a nature to arouse only slight sexual pleasure.

3. A sufficient reason may justify them, always PROVIDED THERE IS NO SERIOUS DANGER OF CONSENT to the pleasure which may arise.

APPLICATIONS

Let us try to apply this principle to concrete cases.

1. Dr. A. studies anatomy and treats women in his practice. Occasionally, the nature of his actions causes complete or nearly complete pleasure, to which he refuses consent. Does he sin?

   a) From his own nature, and from what he does, he is seriously excited.
   b) The action would be a mortal sin without a reason, but
   c) his vocation of curing human ills gives him a sufficient reason. He commits no sin.

2. Mary B. is a mature art student who has progressed so far that, in order to continue, she must study the nude form. She is frequently excited, but refuses consent. She commits no sin.

3. Joan B., her younger sister, aged 17, is also a budding artist. She decides to study the nude with her sister. She too experiences serious excitation to which she refuses consent. She sins mortally if there is no reason at this stage to study the nude, venially if there is a reason but it is used a little too soon.

4. Joe, a boy of 14, finds that in bathing he experiences slight sexual pleasure (no consent). He commits no sin. If he touches himself out of curiosity, venial sin is committed.

5. Sadie, aged 15, reads through a picture magazine which has a number of "lightly clad" illustrations. Out of curiosity she looks at them deliberately, with a light venereal pleasure to which she does not consent. She commits a venial sin.

6. Jack, 17, and Mae, 16, go to a Friday night dance. Though the dances are not suggestive, they both experience some sexual pleasure, to which they refuse to consent. *No sin!* Ordinary dancing is a legitimate form of recreation.

7. Henry, 17, and Isabelle, 16, go out on a date. They indulge in extensive petting, saying that they want to express affection and protesting to themselves that they do not want the sex pleasure resulting. They sin mortally. There is no good reason for these stimulating acts, which are the normal preliminaries of the marriage act.

8. Mike, 21, and Josephine, 20, are to be married in three months. They are very frequently alone; they like to walk arm-in-arm, to hold hands, to embrace on meeting and kiss at parting. Josephine likes to rest her head on Mike's shoulder, and he likes to put his arm around her waist. Sometimes they experience some sexual pleasure, but they do not seek it, being determined to reserve these pleasures for their marriage. They commit no sin at all. They have every right to express decent love. If, however, they indulge in passionate kissing, embracing and petting, they sin seriously, no less than Henry and Isabelle above. About two weeks before their wedding, both Mike and Josephine read an important book on the duties of marriage. Some of the necessary information violently excites them, against their will. They commit no sin. They are obtaining necessary knowledge.

9. Sylvester, aged 16, finds himself excited on all sorts of occasions. He is excited when he sees a girl take out a compact, or walk along the street in modest dress, when he rides his bike, when wrestling in the school gym, when swimming with boys his age, etc., etc. He should ignore all this. He cannot go through life with eyes closed, nor can he be expected to live as a hermit. Sylvester may be suffering from some psychological or moral problem. He should consult a priest. Parents will do well to suggest this to him.

10. Marie experiences sexual arousal in the dressing room with the other girls, against her will. She should learn not to be too curious, but should not be

worried about seeing the bodies of those of her own sex. Even if her curiosity is a bit excessive, it is at most a venial sin.

11. Jim, aged 14, has been concerned with sexual curiosity and temptations for some time, and his dad is straightening things out. During the instruction Jim experiences excitation. Must he stop his father? No, he is obtaining necessary information and training. He must, of course, refuse consent to the sexual excitement.

12. Bill, aged 10, is sick, and his sickness demands that he expose himself to his parents, nurse and doctor. Trained in modesty, Bill is shy about this. His shyness, however, is so severe that he becomes anxious and worried. He should be quietly told that this is false modesty and that no fault whatsoever is involved.

We think this principle is now quite clear. It is the one that is most frequently to be applied in daily life. We would chance the statement that most thoughts and a large portion of the actions which worry adolescents are immodest (leading to lust) rather than impure (actually lustful thoughts and acts). Most of the movies and the pictures in newspapers and magazines that disturb them, can be judged on this principle. We can venture further and say that a large percentage of the actions which cause concern are at most venial sins. Help these adolescents form a clear conscience in these matters!

If any person in the above circumstances becomes worried about *consent,* he can settle his doubt in either of two ways. First, he can ask himself whether he whispers a brief prayer when such feelings arise, for no one can pray for God's help and sin mortally at the same time. Secondly, if he is wise, he will leave off even legitimate activities occasionally just to show himself, and God, that he does not do these things *in order to enjoy* sexual pleasure, but for the *good reason* he has.

It is easy to see that this principle will depend a great deal on the degree of passion in the nature of each person; and this itself will vary as the person grows older. The rough applications of the principle must be worked out by each one for himself. Such applications, especially at first, should be presented to a confessor for approval. A penitent's knowledge of this principle will help the confessor tremendously, and will help the penitent understand the confessor's decision. However, one must take care not to apply one's own norms to others. It is quite possible that others are more, or less, excitable than oneself.

MODESTY CONCERNING OTHERS

The Fourth Moral Principle considers the danger of causing lust or sexual pleasure in others: *Any deliberate action which may arouse sex pleasure, whether voluntary or involuntary, in another, is a mortal or venial sin, or no sin at all, depending on the sexually stimulating nature of the action in proportion to the reason for acting.* Or we might phrase it thus: *Any deliberate action which might cause, or help, another person to sin (on Principles One, Two or Three) is a mortal or venial sin or no sin at all, depending on the amount of danger in proportion to the reason for acting.*

Before discussing this principle we take it for granted that there is no evil intention. If a person really desires to stir lust in another, his intention is evil and he sins seriously even though he does not succeed in his purpose. A girl, for example, who would wear a "French bathing suit" *in order to stir lustful attention* would sin seriously even though, as a matter of fact, her appearance inspired only disgust. She would sin just as seriously *in intention* if she donned a formless raincoat with the purpose of causing lust. Even modest attire does not change an evil purpose. Anyone who has such an evil intention knows he is sinning, without the application of this principle.

Granting that there is no evil intention in our actions, this Fourth Principle holds because we have obligations to our neighbor. We may not do as we please if what we do is a danger to his soul's salvation. Acts which endanger the spiritual life of another are acts of scandal, and are forbidden because love for our neighbor demands that we do not induce or help him to sin. This principle especially concerns modesty in dress, and those actions which are done in company with others.

As we did in the Third Principle, we must consider here the connection of an action with the arousal of lust or sexual pleasure in another and the reason for performing the action.

The Connection of the Action with Sexual Pleasure

The actions which might cause sins of impurity or immodesty in another are sufficiently indicated in the list above (pp. 89-90). That is, it is sinful to cause, or help, a person to sin by violating any of the preceding three moral principles. Therefore, if it would be sinful for John to look at obscene pictures (Third Principle), it would be equally sinful for Joseph to give such pictures to John. If heavy petting is seriously sinful for George (Third Principle), it would be equally sinful for Mary to permit such indecencies (Fourth Principle) even though she could honestly say that the actions did not stir her passions. Again, if listening to "dirty jokes" for the humor is venially sinful for James, telling him such jokes is also a venial sin. In other words, if a person's action is so stimulating as to be rather certain to arouse lust in someone else (Principle I or II), or even full involuntary sexual pleasure (Principle III), that action is a mortal sin (Principle IV) unless there is some serious reason to excuse it. If the action is but slightly tempting, it is a venial sin, unless some adequate reason is present. To understand why this is true, consult the portion of this work which considers the psychology of sexual arousal (pp. 122 ff.).

Those Who May Be Scandalized

It is especially important to consider the various groups of people who might be tempted by one's actions to sin. The first group comprises those who are looking for opportunities to sin. Such people are scandalized by others in the same way as the Pharisees of old. They blame others for giving them the occasion of sinning, despite the fact that they are searching for the occasions. No one has any obligation to avoid giving opportunities to such people. They must solve their own problems. For example, should a young man look with obvious lust on a young woman even though her dress and actions are conventionally modest, she has no obligation to change her manner of dress or behavior.

The second group is composed of ordinary people who try to live a chaste life. Divine charity obliges us to avoid giving them occasions for sin. Therefore, any action which would bring some well-intentioned person to sin, or to grave danger of sin, would itself be sinful. For example, it would ordinarily be a serious sin to tell a luridly obscene story to any normal unmarried person.

The last group includes those who, however well-intentioned, are weak regarding their observance of the Sixth Commandment. This group is composed of children, adolescents, and any others who are known to be especially liable to sin. Extraordinary precautions must be taken with this group. For example, it would be seriously sinful to take a 14-year-old boy to an indecent movie, even though the presentation would not greatly disturb an adult. Again, once a boy or girl knows that some action will stir lust in his or her partner on a date, the performance of that action will be sinful unless a real reason exists which excuses it.

The Justifying Reason

The reason which might justify otherwise immodest acts must be in proportion to the effect. It would take a weighty reason to justify a very stimulating action, a lesser reason to justify a less stimulating one. For example, ordinarily it would be at most venially sinful to give a slightly off-color book to a friend. However, if one is asked for the book, the avoidance of a quarrel might be a sufficiently justifying reason. Such a reason, however, would not justify the loan of the book to an adolescent. Again, it would be mortally sinful for a young woman to appear nude before a man; not at all sinful for her to do so before a doctor for necessary treatment or examination. To make these things clear for the Fourth Principle, we shall summarize them in schema form just as we did for Principle III:

1. Acts which might lead another to sin (according to the First, Second or Third Principles) depend:
   a) on the stimulating nature of the act;
   b) on the excitability of the individual concerned (Pharasaical, ordinary, or weak).

2. These acts, performed without a good reason, are:
   a) mortally sinful if they are such as to lead, or help, another to sin mortally (by violating any of the first three principles);
   b) venially sinful if they are such as to lead him to venial sin.

3. A sufficient reason may justify these actions, provided THERE IS NO EVIL INTENTION IN THE ACTIONS.

APPLICATIONS OF THE FOURTH PRINCIPLE

1. Kate, a young woman, prepares for bed each evening with lights on and blinds up. Her room faces the homes opposite, where she knows several teen-age boys live with their parents. She insists she has no evil intentions. Does she sin?

a) Her actions are certainly stimulating to any male onlooker, and the individuals concerned are ordinary flesh-and-blood young men, that is, certainly excitable in this case.

b) There can be no justifying reason. It would take but a moment to pull the blinds or to turn off the light. Kate sins mortally.

2. Mrs. B. has suddenly been asked by her 14-year-old son all about the facts of human generation. She knows her answers may be dangerous, but, taking what precautions she can, she replies frankly and fully to all his questions. Does she sin?

a) Her words may be stimulating because of the nature of the subject, and her boy is in the weak class.

b) She has a perfectly justifying reason. If she loses this opportunity, he may obtain his information from evil sources. She does not sin, and should not worry. Indeed she is performing an act of virtue, one of her parental duties.

3. Maureen, aged 17, fancies herself the "desirable" clinging-vine type. She wears the extreme in evening dress and swim suits. She "melts" over her date, allowing little room between the two in his car. She experiences no passion herself, and claims she merely wishes to indicate her friendship for him. If she realizes what her actions are doing to her escort (and she should be made to realize it), she sins seriously because the stimulation of her attire and actions have no justifying reasons.

4. Leonard, aged 21, possesses some pin-ups which however are not of an extremely vile nature. He shows them to his friends of the same age. Does he sin? Since there is some danger here, though hardly serious danger, he sins venially unless he has some proportionate reason. If he should show them to his excitable younger brother, he would come closer to serious sin.

5. Lydia is an attractive girl of 17. Her uncle, the big, bluff type, always gives her a hearty hug when he passes and indulges in other slaps, pats, etc. Lydia sometimes suspects that all this is not in fun. Does she sin in allowing the familiarities? Granting that Lydia does not encourage these things, she does not sin because she has a sufficient reason: his relationship to her, the presence of other members of the family, the scene which would be created if she "stood on her dignity," etc. Perhaps some older person would do well to show disapproval.

6. Mary, aged 19, likes and wears dresses which, while not excessively revealing, are of the more extreme fashion. Her sin is probably only venial. If she had a good reason—for example, if it were *really* impossible to get more modest dresses—she would be excused.

7. Jim, aged 16, indulges in antics in the nude while in the dressing room with other boys. He has no evil intention of stirring passions. There are younger boys present and also (he knows) some who are more excitable than he. He sins mortally or venially, depending on how much he realizes the danger into which he is thrusting the others.

8. Dolores, while her dress is by no means immodest, is careless about knee-crossing, her method of walking, her swirling dancing, etc. She knows the boys are looking on with some glee. She sins mortally or venially, depending on the degree of immodesty in her acts. She has no excuse for ignoring the proprieties. If she did these things deliberately to stir passion, it would be serious immediately.

9. Joe knows that some of his friends are rather excitable in sex matters. Yet, in the boys' dressing room, he does not hesitate to undress before them. He commits no fault. He cannot avoid every possibility, and they have the obligation to guard themselves or to develop the proper attitude.

10. Lil plays basketball on a Catholic high school team. Their gym dress is approved. Despite that she wonders about some of the gallery, and she decides to quit the team. She need not do so, since she has no obligation to avoid being the object of *such* eyes. They must look to themselves.

There are many more problems on this principle. Some will be found in the discussion aids. You will probably have many problems yourself. Try to apply the principle and check your applications with others.

DOUBLE STANDARD?

Many people have said that the Church teaches a double moral standard, one for men and another for women. This is not true. The four moral principles above apply *in their full force to both sexes.* Lust is a serious sin in either sex and demands the same expiation before God's seat of justice. However, because of the different constitutions of the sexes, certain difficulties are stronger in one sex than in the other and need more care. Men usually have more difficulty and must be more guarded regarding chastity in the strict sense and in modesty of eyes and touch. Women must give more attention to the whole field of modesty, particularly modesty concerning others. In the long run the difficulties of the Sixth and Ninth Commandments come out about even. If boys and girls will feel responsible for each other, there will be far less trouble in this field which has so obsessed the modern mind.

REASON FOR THE MORAL PRINCIPLES

Why do the Four Moral Principles in these two chapters point out what is sinful? Because venereal pleasure is for the married alone. Therefore, outside of marriage, *to enjoy such pleasure, desire it, think with approval of it as present, or take a chance on causing it, is a sin.* Let us explain this by an example from the Fifth Commandment. No one may take a life unjustly. Therefore, it is a sin to *shoot* a man (including yourself). It is a sin to *desire* to shoot him, or to *delight in his murder.* It is also sinful to *chance* shooting a man without a justifying reason. You may have every right to hunt for squirrels, but not in a city park on Sunday afternoon when all the strollers are there, for then, if your stray bullet kills a man, you are responsible. You might, however, shoot at an escaped tiger on the city streets even though a wild shot might hurt someone. In this case, you have a reason (saving others) for allowing this to happen against your will. It is the same with sexual pleasure outside of marriage. *You may not enjoy it, desire it, or think of it as present. You may not, without a good reason, do anything that might cause it even involuntarily in yourself or others.*

This chapter is perhaps the most difficult in the entire book. And yet it is probably the most important because the matter it contains is so little understood by Catholics and non-Catholics alike. However, it is not so very hard. Here is a re-statement of the principles you have learned:

3. *To take a chance of producing sexual pleasure in oneself without a reason is mortal or venial depending on how close the chance is. A reason may excuse from all sin or make a serious matter light.*

4. *To chance causing lust or unwanted sexual pleasure in another without a reason is mortal or venial, or no sin at all, depending on what is done. A good reason may excuse from all sin or make a serious matter light.*

Throughout this chapter we have been concerned with judging the *sinfulness* of actions. One word remains to be said. There is the chance that some reader may think, "Oh, I can allow this to happen, it is *only* a venial sin!" True, it may be only a venial sin, but that too is an offense against God which should be avoided as far as is humanly possible. Besides that, we should not be content with avoiding sin, but should strive earnestly to practice virtue. Therefore, let adolescents fully understand these moral principles, and grasp the differences that have been laid down; but once they know them, let them face resolutely forward and determine to pursue virtue and not be content with merely the minimum—avoiding mortal sin. The *good* automobile driver should be able to gauge exactly the number of inches between his speeding car and a precipice; but he remains a *safe* driver only when he keeps as far from the precipice as possible.

CASES FOR SOLUTION

1. Jack and Jill, both 16, go for a hike with their "gang." When lunch is being prepared, Jack takes a choice morsel and is just about to eat it when Jill snatches it from him and runs. He gives chase, catches her, and engages in a tussle to get it back. As he does so, he experiences some sexual pleasure to which he gives an emphatic "*No!*" He continues the tussle and finally triumphs. Has he sinned? Should this experience give him a warning for the future? In a similar case afterward, could he do the same without sin? Would it be *better* not to do so?

2. Kathy is beautiful. A contest is being staged for Miss Squeedunk of 19—, with attractive prizes. She decides to enter. The contestants will, of course, wear bathing suits. May she enter? (Consider the process: line-up, parade, onlookers, judges, elimination, measuring tapes, etc.) Does she sin if she enters? If so, how seriously?

3. Mazie wants to be a photographer's model. The pictures will be published in popular magazines. Modeling will entail various kinds of undress and posing for pin-up pictures. May she take the job? Suppose she can get a job modeling clothing which really *clothes,* and only an occasional

job of the other kind will turn up. Will that make any difference?

4. John, aged 14, decides to get a look into the girls' dressing room at the gym. He knows he should not do so and he expects to get quite a sexual thrill. Yet he sees nothing to excite him as there are individual dressing compartments. Does he sin? How seriously? *(Mortally: Principle I.)*

5. Marjorie wants to be a majorette in her high school band. May she? Discuss the implications in the usual dress for such a function.

6. Dick and Charlotte are acrobatic dancers. The normal amount of clothing interferes with their work. May they continue in this as a profession? Should there be some *norms* in this matter? Are there, in fact, any such norms? Does the intention of these dancers (or aerialists, circus performers, etc.), to show skill rather than exhibit bodies, make a difference? *(Yes.)*

7. James, aged 17, goes to a theater which has a stage presentation in addition to the movie. Some of the jokes are indecent and one or two of the dances suggestive. Must he leave? Might it be better to leave? Discuss the proper procedure if he may remain.

8. Joanne, aged 20, is advised by her doctor to get some sun. She dons a very brief costume and climbs to the roof, which seems safe from prying eyes. After some time she notices a head in the distance which has managed by elaborate effort to obtain a view of the "scenery." Must she give up her sun-bathing?

9. Henry, aged 16, goes to a public high school. After school some of the boys gather to tell various suggestive jokes. Henry occasionally is forced by circumstances to listen and cannot help laughing (after all, they *are* funny). They are very stimulating, but he rejects any incipient venereal pleasure. Does he sin? On another occasion he deliberately listens and joins in. Again he rejects the pleasure. Does he sin this time? He finds out after a while that these stories linger in his mind and cause temptation to which he sometimes gives consent. If he listens by choice, is he responsible for these temptations? Must he consider the

stories an occasion of sin which he must avoid?

10. Elaine, aged 17, has an illness which demands a thorough physical examination. May she present herself to a male doctor? *(You know the answer is "Yes," but apply the Principle to discover the reason for your answer.)*

11. Ruth plays basketball with a team which wears an acceptably modest uniform. Yet she plays to draw the eyes of the gallery. If she only wants to be "attractive," does she sin? If she wants to stir lustful attention, does she sin?

NOTE: In each case, tell what principle is involved, in your opinion, and go through it point by point. Please do not jump to conclusions from your general knowledge! Go back to the cases proposed in the text of this chapter and apply your norms to them detail by detail.

QUESTIONS AND DISCUSSION AIDS

1. What is modesty?

2. Phrase Principle III in one of its three forms.

3. Decide this case on the Principle: Bill, aged 16, looks through the New York Times Magazine Section. There are numerous underwear advertisements. Bill looks at them curiously. He experiences a very light sexual thrill to which he does not consent. Does he sin mortally? Venially? Not at all? Why? *(Remember the procedure: What is done? What is its connection with unwanted venereal pleasure for this person? What is the reason?)*

4. What teen-age activities that seem immodest worry you? Try to apply the yardstick of this Third Principle to them.

5. What is Principle IV? Why should we take care not to cause lust or sex pleasure in others? Have we any obligations to them?

6. Discuss immodesty in dress. In our modern costumes, just what is immodest in your opinion (that is, tending to arouse lust or venereal pleasure in an ordinary person)? Concrete cases will come to mind. Discuss them and try to

arrive at a decision. Is immodesty in dress the only difficulty which comes under this principle? What about touches, storytelling, etc.?

7. Must every occasion of sin to another be avoided in one's actions? There are three kinds of people: the weak, the ordinary, and the ill-intentioned. Which ones must you safeguard?

8. Does your last answer indicate any obligations toward children and adolescents (weak)? Will this curtail activity which, though not ordinarily scandalous, might cause scandal in children? Does this make the divisions of the Legion of Decency movie list reasonable? Does scandal mean shocked surprise or does it mean inducement to sin? (*Fourth Principle.*)

9. Do Catholics defend a double standard of morality? Why does it, at times, appear that they do?

10. Is our example from the Fifth Commandment a good parallel for the Sixth? Do you understand now why our moral standard is so high?

Chapter IX

Emotional Attitudes Toward Sex and Sex Education

WHAT IS EMOTION?

The modern usage of the words "emotion" and "passion" is rather vague, so we shall give our own definitions. The sexual or venereal reaction is not what is meant here by emotion. That reaction we shall always term "sexual passion." Thus (as will be explained in the psychological section), the physical passion of sex is an automatic reflex action similar to the secretion of saliva or the mechanism of a blush. Emotion, in our sense, has little or nothing to do with sexual pleasure. Emotion is best explained by the word "feeling." It is how we *feel* about or react to a problem or person, whether this be a feeling of pride, content, anxiety, worry, joy, fear, or a hundred others. Emotions have a physical basis; they are felt in the body. They may be *accompanied by* sexual passion, but one is not the other. St. Thomas numbers desire, love, joy, fear, hate, sadness, despair, anger, etc., among the emotions. We may add to the list feelings of exhilaration, anticipation, shame, jealousy, envy, worry, anxiety, loathing, etc. Consequently, for a parent to have the correct emotional outlook on marriage, sex, and the duty of sex education, is to have habitually the correct feeling toward these things. To give a child the correct emotional outlook on sex and marriage is to give him the right feelings toward them.

EMOTIONAL ATTITUDE OF PARENTS TO SEX EDUCATION

It is difficult to list the correct emotions toward this problem without repeating many things already mentioned. We have paused at nearly every point to indicate the correct emotional attitude. However, it may be helpful to list in this section, for additional emphasis, some of the more important emotions.

Parents should feel joyful *responsibility* for the correct sex education of their children; joyful because the successful meeting of this obligation will bring genuine happiness to themselves and their children. This sense of responsibility should *not* beget *despair, worry,* or *excessive anxiety.*[1] Face the duty confident that you can perform it with a little preparation, good common sense, and of course, the help of prayer. Try to manifest this sureness to your child. This you will succeed in doing if you courageously answer each question. When it is impossible to satisfy your child's needs immediately, at least show a willingness to satisfy them later by looking up the matter in the meantime. Be *kind, patient,* and even *long-suffering* with your child's problems. While not demanding confidences (the child, and particularly the adolescent, wants a corner of his personality to himself), try to invite such confidence by a calm *sympathy* with all his problems. Show, above all, that you are never *afraid* of a problem even though time or circumstance may force you to put it off temporarily. Your approach should be *frank, sincere, matter-of-fact,* and without any indication of *shame, disgust* or *distaste.* If carried out sympathetically, good chastity education will prove a bond of intimacy between parent and child, will bring a great deal of satisfaction to both, and will help mature the character of all concerned.

---

1. Throughout this chapter each suitable or unsuitable emotion will be printed in italics. After reading the somewhat involved presentation, you need only glance over the italicized words to see which emotions are desirable and which are to be avoided in each case.

Emotion and Children's Sins

Should your children fall into some sexual sin, show *sadness, but not shock. Encourage* them to sorrow and Confession, and show your *confidence* in their ability to remain chaste. *Compassion* and *sympathy* are the chief emotions called for in this case. Refer back to Chapter VI, p. 65-66, for a very important section on emotions and children's sins.

Emotion toward Their Temptations

Show your children that you recognize the struggle they may be facing at any one time and that you are "rooting on the sidelines" for them. Never show surprise that your teen-agers are struggling with "bad thoughts." Help them! Be ready (but not "trigger happy") with good advice. Above all, never laugh at their problems as though these were unimportant. To your children, they are very important. You may laugh *with* your children, showing them there is no need for worry, but never *at* them.[2]

EMOTIONAL ATTITUDES FOR CHILDREN

To engender in your children the correct emotional attitudes toward the body, sex, marriage and parenthood, you must yourself have the correct attitudes, because tone of voice and many unconscious acts do more to educate children than mere words. If you have any wrong attitude, try to change it, or at least avoid giving it to your children. What we have to say in the following pages should be a guide not only for children's emotions but also, in general, for parents' emotions.

---

2. For the way to use comradely laughter, cf. a beautiful sex instruction reported by Maura Laverty in *Never No More* (Longmans, Green, New York, 1942), pp. 61ff. This instruction is worth study for emotions, words, and the wise thought behind it.

Attitude toward the Body

A good Catholic should respect his body because it was created by God. Every part of it is good! Since the body is good, to be *happy* in the possession of a healthy, beautiful or handsome body is well within the bounds of Christian modesty for boys and girls, and reasonable adornment is not only permissible but laudable. Such natural pride should be spiritualized, since the body is a temple of the Holy Spirit and a member of the Body of Christ. On the other hand, it is silly and a waste of time to complain about the stings of the flesh as some young people do. After all, temptation is a challenge, a test. Young people should be more *proud* of passing that test than of making the football team, leading the class, or being Queen of the May. Because they have accepted that challenge, they ought to resent the activities of those who hold up the impure and lustful as models.

Attitude toward One's Own Sex

Boys should be glad to be boys, and girls should be glad to be girls. No good of any kind can come from wishing the opposite. Boys should strive to be virile and masculine in the true sense of manliness. Girls should be proud of their womanly virtues and feminine traits. Neither sex should envy the other because neither sex is, in reality, superior to the other. Though we must defend the right of a father to be the head of the family, each sex has its own proper superiorities. The sexes are not opposed to each other, nor are they in a contest for supremacy. They are complementary, and fill out each other's needs. They fit together in every respect, like the right and left hand. It is a parental duty to indicate, by word and example, the qualities which make a masculine man and a feminine woman. Members of each sex should learn to take in stride their bodily and psychological difficulties (menstruation, muscular weakness, and temptation to immodesty in dress for the girl; seminal emission, physical temptation, and temptation to immodesty of the eyes for the boy). These are a challenge to virtue and self-control.

For each sex there should always be a sense of modesty and reserve even among themselves. Dressing rooms are always places where Catholics are recognized as such. There should, however, be no feeling of shame in these places. True shame should only be connected with sins of impurity or immodesty. A girl should feel ashamed to appear on a beach in immodest attire; a boy should be ashamed of a frankly "roving" eye; but neither sex should be ashamed of dressing or undressing among themselves, when necessary.

Attitude toward Sexuality

The proper emotional attitude toward the sexual functions and their possible holy use in marriage is well summed up in two words, *reverent wonder.* The sexual powers are a trust from God, something to be treasured, something to cause wonder at His goodness, something to be carefully guarded and used ever according to His law—in marriage only (cf. Chapter VI, pp. 59-60). Since they provide the possibility of the highest physical expression of human love; since, by their use, one can co-operate with God Himself in bringing forth children for His Kingdom—these powers can only be received with awe and a determination to preserve them inviolate at all costs. For this reason, shame, hate, loathing or disgust must never be associated with sexual acts in marriage. At the opposite extreme, there should be no "smutty," *lustful anticipation.* Through parental instruction, the child and adolescent should never be given the idea that the sexual union is a dirty, shameful business, a defiling kind of "fun," an act of forbidden pleasure somehow justified in marriage. The child should be imbued with this attitude: "When and if I marry, such sacred pleasure will be mine as a reward for a virtuous act. Until then I am determined, with God's help, to remain virginal." A normal, *unimaginative anticipation* should be as natural as to say: "When I am twenty-one I may vote," and "When I am old enough I may smoke."

Especially in the realm of purity does reverence play a specific role. Purity essentially involves a reverent attitude toward the mystery of love between man and woman, a consciousness that the sphere of sex is a realm which should be approached only with a special sanction of God, which should fill us with awe. Purity is incompatible with a general arrogant attitude toward being, whether it assumes a frivolous, cynical character or a blunt, smug familiarity with the mystery of the cosmos.

Purity demands respect for the beloved, respect for his body, respect for the great mysterious union of two souls in one flesh, respect for the mystery of the becoming of a new human being.

In education for purity, the role of the general attitude of reverence cannot be overestimated. We cannot expect of a young man a right attitude in the domain of sex if we neglect the education of reverence in general.[3]

Attitude toward Temptation and Sin

Once our youth have appreciated the positive beauty and value of sexuality, it will be easier for them to avoid *violent fear* of sexual temptation. Excessive fear of temptation tends to fix the mind on what is to be avoided, which would certainly be an unhealthy state of affairs. However, there may well be a *reasonable fear* of offending God, of losing the treasure of virginity, and

---

3. Von Hildebrand, Dietrich, "The Role of Reverence in Education," in *Lumen Vitae,* 1949 (IV), p. 636. Quoted with permission of the publisher.

hence fear of the temptation which may cause the fall. A *quiet fear* of this sort is healthy because it helps one to avoid the danger. To this quiet fear it is proper to add a sensible *confidence* in God, who does not allow temptation above our strength, and who gives us help to overcome it *if we ask Him* (cf. *1 Cor.* 10:13). Many adolescents become very *anxious* about the new feelings and imaginations they experience. They fear that they are different from their comrades, and believe, at times, that they are born wicked because of such unbidden thoughts and feelings. In some cases, a boy (or girl) might consider the possibility of having gone insane! Young people will breathe a sigh of relief when you explain how normal and universal are these experiences at their age. Should they wonder why these new disturbances occur, it is well to explain the glandular changes in their bodies and the psychological changes in their minds which are but indications of their rapidly approaching maturity (cf. Chapters X and XI). With this background of information, boys and girls will soon learn to face these temptations calmly, with the determination to remain chaste, and with confidence in their own good will and God's help. To prevent both excessive worry and sudden lapses into sin due to surprise temptations, give them either of these two cautions as mottoes: "Don't look for trouble, but don't be surprised when it comes," or "Be ready but not anxious."

Neither a single sin nor a habit of sin should cause *despair.* An individual fall should make one *sorrowful* but a great deal more wise. A fall indicates one's weakness and points out where the danger is to be faced and avoided. Never let a child think his sin is unforgivable, or is too evil to confess. Every sin and every evil habit can be forgiven and conquered with courage and trust in God. Though one should be ashamed of sin, the shame must not make it impossible to confess the sin and conquer it in the future.

A very good attitude for a child to have in matters

of purity and modesty is a willing obedience to confessors and parents, even without complete understanding of the reasons. Regarding obedience, parents have a double problem. They must teach obedience and yet give reasons. In the beginning, a child must be taught simply to obey. He is too young to understand an explanation. Gradually reasons must be given. The child must understand that parents always have a reason, even if it is not given at the time. He must learn to obey: first, from habit; second, for the reason given; third, from the fact that there *is* a reason even if it is not given or understood. A youngster who demands a reason should be answered if possible. If the reason will not be understood, obedience must nevertheless be exacted. Beware, however, of giving a command from mere whim. *Always have a reason.* As the years go on, more and more reasons must be given, for the child must eventually learn to take over his own thinking.

A great delicacy is needed in dealing with adolescents. The adolescent *needs* to practice some obedience. He will even *desire* it. Yet, at the same time, he wants more freedom to judge for himself. Therefore, keep the reins but handle them lightly. You should be able to free him from restraint by 18, *if* you have given enough reasons to enable him to judge for himself, at least with advice and counsel.

Attitudes toward the Other Sex

The relations between the sexes ought to be characterized by mutual *enjoyment, liking* and *respect. Chivalry, responsibility, courtesy,* together with a *sensible caution* and *reasonable modesty,* should mark all their meetings and fun together. All boys and girls must feel responsible for the purity of their friends of the other sex. To have an enjoyable evening without endangering one another, should be a challenge they willingly accept. Such an enjoyable and sinless evening can easily be had if young people plan the date or party in advance. In this planning, parents can help by their suggestions for fun, by occasionally offering their services as cook, and by their "in and out" presence at any gathering. Above all, they must make their children's friends welcome in their home.[4]

Young people occasionally face the problem of "following the crowd." If an evil suggestion is made, they dare not show their distaste or shame at the very thought. As St. Augustine remarks, Catholics are sometimes "ashamed of being ashamed."[5] This would be false shame. On occasion, Catholics must show that they are different. It is high time that they began to set Christian patterns in their own groups instead of mimicking the paganism around them. Parents must encourage these Christian patterns more strongly.

Attitude toward Marriage

Frivolous ideas of marriage should never be expressed in the family circle. This does not exclude humorous jokes on the difficulties of marriage, for how could anyone manage the rough spots without a sense of humor? Nevertheless, marriage is a lofty and serious affair, a noble state of life, and should be treated as such.

It is quite appropriate to discuss some important family matters in the children's presence. The *seriousness* of discussion and care in arriving at a decision will make it clear that marriage is a weighty undertaking. Again, there is no reason why family secrets may not be discussed before the children. Children love a secret and will be willing to keep one entrusted to them—especially if they have been well trained in internal discipline from the beginning. If they fail, they should be punished for their disloyalty to the family. There are indeed "sacred and intimate things which belong to family life, and are but sparingly shared with

---

4. For further helpful suggestions, cf. Lord, Daniel, S. J., *Some Notes for the Guidance of Parents* (The Queen's Work, St. Louis, 1944)
5. *Confessions of St. Augustine* (Sheed and Ward, New York, 1943), II, 9, p. 37.

others."[6] Incidentally, one of these sacred things is the expected arrival of a new baby.

Almost all of married life is lived in the presence of the children. Hence, all the *expressions of love* between husband and wife must not be given in their absence. On the other hand, *gushy sentimentality* is equally out of place. Affection cannot be "acted out" for children, it must be real and unassuming. The tone of voice means more than the words. Children clearly perceive artificial tones for what they are—sheer pretense. Each parent must examine himself to see how much sentiment he can in reality express for his partner. After such examination, honest and unassuming ritual should be incorporated into all home life: a kiss before going to work and upon returning, courtesy, respect, politeness between husband and wife, etc. The father should definitely assume his role as head and ruler of the household. The mother, on her part, ought to exemplify and assert her place as "queen of hearts" in the home (cf. encyclical *On Christian Marriage*).

It is wise to try to avoid quarrels, or to hide them from the children. Yet few households give enough privacy for private discussions of this sort. Moreover, should the disagreement arise before the children, the solution should also take place in their presence. By this solution we do not mean a sentimental "patching up." If both husband and wife have been at fault, there ought to be a mutual and honest giving in. If one alone is guilty, an honest admission and apology are in order. It may be hard to step off the pedestal before your children, to show that you are of common clay. Yet they will learn to respect you all the more as a humble and brave person, since only a coward refuses to admit an obvious fault. From such give and take, children will absorb valuable lessons for later life.

When the attitudes listed in this section are present in a home, children will absorb them easily, and will

6. King, *op. cit.*, p. 23.

need scarcely any formal instruction on the sacred and noble character of Matrimony.

Attitude toward Parenthood

Granted that no other vocation has been chosen, parenthood should be *pleasantly anticipated* by both boys and girls. When parental example is on the above bases, children will certainly deem it a *beautiful* and *wonderful* vocation to have children, to love and nourish them, to help them unfold their personalities, and to build up in them strong Christian characters.

The Girl's Attitude: Every girl, as Pius XII beautifully reminds us, should *desire* to be a mother, either in fact or in spirit.[7] However, this desire must be realistic, for it is as disastrous to have a wholly *romantic* picture as to have a wholly *grim* one. *Tremendous fear* of the burden and danger of giving birth to and raising a family should be as much avoided as *idyllic pictures* of the beauties and consolations of motherhood unmixed with trials. As part of their training for this probable future role, girls should be taught to bear patiently the inconveniences of menstruation. It is a small payment for their wonderful development and function. All references to the "curse of Eve" and the "plague of women" are out of place (cf. Maura Laverty, *op. cit.,* p. 63). Girls should not ordinarily be allowed to plead sickness during the time of menstruation unless, of course, the reaction is severe (in which case it might be wise to consult a doctor).

Toward having children, the best and most realistic attitude is that pointed out by Christ Himself: "A woman about to give birth has sorrow, because her hour has come. But when she has brought forth the child, she no longer remembers the anguish for her joy that a man is born into the world" (*John* 16:21). To accentuate the pains without the joy or the joy without the

---

7. Cf. *Women's Duties in Social and Political Life,* Paulist Press, New York, 1945.

pains is equally unrealistic. *The labor of travail is worthwhile, hard work:* this describes the proper attitude toward childbirth.

Some modern doctors insist that *fear* of pain creates all the more pain.[8] Though many mothers may be skeptical of such medical opinion, it has been shown that the pain of childbirth is definitely less if *recognized and faced.* What pain there is may well be made a sacrifice of expiation for sin, and of prayer for the child. A young mother who anticipated, and had a very difficult delivery (and who for medical reasons could not be anaesthetized), resolved to offer her pain for the souls in Purgatory. Though she admitted she was not very brave at the time, who will say that her initial offering of sacrifice was not received? Confidence in modern medical care should eliminate most of the fears of childbirth. More women by far die while pleasure-driving in automobiles than while bringing new life into the world!

Proper attitudes should similarly be engendered toward the nursing of infants. Children, especially the younger ones, should not be forbidden to see mother breast-feeding the baby. Moderns are accustomed to all kinds of immodesty, yet are prudish in their view of this beautiful act. A curious inversion of values indeed! A mother should be *proud* of her duty and function. It should never be considered *disgusting* or *shameful.* Many doctors are returning to the age-old conviction: all factors being favorable, no bottle or formula can take the place of a healthy mother's milk.[9]

In all these matters the example of the mother is everything. When she is "expecting," she should be proud and joyful, and all the family should rejoice in the family "secret." Her noble, happy, realistic attitude, not only

8. Cf. Read, Grantly Dick, *Childbirth without Fear,* Harper and Brothers, New York, 1946.
9. Cf. Rice, Frederick W., M. D., "The Function of Lactation," in *The Family Today* (N. C. W. C. Press, Washington, D. C., 1944), pp. 96ff.; also Carrel, Alexis, "Breast-feeding for Babies," in *Reader's Digest* (June, 1939); and Newton, Niles, "Breast-feeding—Psychological Aspects," in *Child-Family Digest* (New Orleans, La., January, 1952), pp. 56ff.

toward giving birth but toward all the duties of motherhood, has more influence than any words she may use.

The Boy's Attitude: The attitude of an adolescent boy toward parenthood should be that it is a *joy* and a *responsibility.* He should know that women suffer pain at childbirth, and that this is normal. But he must not have the idea that a husband should regard such pangs in a *coldly indifferent* light, nor on the other hand *feel guilty* and *remorseful* about them. If his early training causes him to say when he becomes a father, "I'll never allow this to happen to my darling again," it has given him a false view of marriage. Here, too, parental example is paramount. The love, care, respect and consideration a boy has seen his father show toward his pregnant mother mean much more than words. Again, if a father evidences joy in his children, really assists in raising them, takes part in the life of the family, and gives evidences of his careful planning for all, his boys will learn, from their earliest years, the correct attitude toward parenthood. Too many men look on their children as necessary nuisances which their long-suffering wives should control, quiet, and send to bed early. Fathers are parents too! They have the obligation to head their families in all things, including child-training.[10]

QUESTIONS AND DISCUSSION AIDS

1. Is passion the same as emotion? Are emotions good in themselves? (*Yes.*) When is an emotion bad? (*When it is not the one which correctly fits the situation.*) Can emotions be controlled? Can correct emotions be learned? Give examples.

2. What emotions or feelings would you say this book has given you toward the duty of sex education? Do they correspond to the ones we have listed as necessary?

---

10. For attitudes toward children, cf.: *A Mother Looks at Birth Control* (The Queen's Work, St. Louis, 1947); "Are Women a Lost Sex?" in the *Liguorian Magazine* (October, 1947), pp. 433ff.; *Parenthood* (The Queen's Work, St. Louis, 1946); Nutting, Willis, *Parents Are Teachers* (Liturgical Press, Collegeville, Minn., 1949).

3. Should you demand confidences from your children? Why, or why not? Would it be a good idea to tell one child's confidences to the rest of the family? To your husband or wife? Discuss this matter.

4. What circumstances may be used as a reason to defer sex instruction or education? (*Lack of privacy, too busy, etc.*) Should this delay be long?

5. How do you react to a discovery of sin in your child? How should you react? Are you surprised at temptation in yourself or others? Give some concrete cases of "laughing at" and "laughing with" children in their problems.

6. Is it wise to follow up suspicion based on good grounds? Give some example of founded and unfounded suspicions.

7. Do you believe that adolescence is a period for "sowing wild oats" and that nothing can be done about it?

8. Is the body evil? Good? Half and half? Can one be born bad? Is self-adornment unchristian? Why? Why should not a girl wish that she were a boy? (*Boys seldom desire to be girls.*)

9. Is one sex inferior to the other? Discuss this. List the superiorities of each sex side by side. Do you find the same number in each? Is each quality of equal value?

10. How, concretely, should your boy or girl act in a dressing room?

11. What common-sense attitude should characterize a boy's or girl's outlook on sexual things in marriage? What are some prevalent false notions? Can you add to our list?

12. Is fear always bad? (*No!*) What kind is? What kind is not? Does violent fear fix temptation? Can you corroborate this from personal experience?

13. How can we use failure to our own advantage? Do you believe this statement, "In education, mistakes are almost as important as success"? Do teachers correct and return papers? Has this any value? Does it suggest the value of correcting behavior, manners, and morals? Is it enough

to point out with a check mark what is wrong, or must reasons and helps be added?

14. Is one child different from another? Are there both resemblances and differences? Will it help a child to understand this?

15. Is there any sin which cannot be forgiven, if one has the proper dispositions?

16. Has obedience any connection with chastity? Should obedience or reasons come first? Should they come together? Or sometimes one, sometimes the other? Are there laws which even adults must obey though they may not understand the reasons? Will it help a child to understand this?

17. What two words crystallize a proper approach to the opposite sex? (*Responsibility and respect.*)

18. Must a Catholic at times be different? How can you answer an objection like this: "But all the kids at school are Catholic and they are doing it!" (*Are* all *doing it? Are they* Catholic *in doing it?*) Do you think parents could organize to prevent this indiscriminate "following the crowd"? (*Apply this to beach and sports wear for girls and boys, late hours, dating, etc.*)

19. A girl of 16 observed her father ogling women on the beach. He turned to her and said, "If you ever wear a bathing suit like that, I'll kill you." Why was she bewildered? Which was more powerful, his example or his words? Will she obey him?

20. Is marriage a serious vocation? Do your actions prove your convictions? Do you agree that quarrels can be kept from children? Can this be done perfectly?

21. Are there family secrets? Would you punish the child who blurted out your monthly income? Would you punish him for talking about his bodily functions except in necessity? About a new baby still months off? Should you?

22. Will it help a girl to face the difficulties of motherhood if you tell her, "Mother went down to death's door for

you"? What is a realistic approach to motherhood? Is embarrassment at obvious pregnancy healthy? Should an expectant mother refuse to be seen in her "condition"? (What a word!) A little girl of 10 was asked, "Wouldn't you like to continue school and be a nurse, or teacher, or career girl"? "No," she answered, "I want to be a mother." Is this a healthy or unhealthy attitude?

23. What is a healthy attitude toward fatherhood? Are many fathers refusing to be parents today?

Chapter X

Psychological Factors In
Catholic Sex Education

Our division between psychological and emotional factors is merely arbitrary. Emotion refers to *feeling* about things, whereas psychology, in our sense, refers to an *understanding* of how the human being reacts in various situations connected with sexual facts. In the previous chapter we explained the proper emotional attitudes toward these problems. In this chapter we shall consider the origin and control of sexual passion, the psychology of love, the psychology of discipline, and the psychology of adolescence.

HOW SEX PASSION ARISES

In general, sexual passion or venereal pleasure: 1) arises from a stimulus of touch, sight, smell, imagination, or any combination of these; 2) arises more quickly in the boy than in the girl, and usually from a different combination of circumstances. Of course, experiences vary almost infinitely, depending on the individuals concerned and the circumstances involved. We list here merely the generally accepted outlines. An individual must not be considered abnormal merely because he does not conform to this composite picture.

Because of our fallen and perverse inclinations sexual feelings are not under the direct control of the will. Sexual passion is an automatic reaction that arises when certain mental or physical stimuli are applied. The reactions are similar to the workings of the digestive organs. The sizzle and aroma of a broiling steak will cause feelings of hunger in a man who was not hungry a moment before. In the same way, romantic imaginations, pictures of nudity, remembered images of beaches, movies and plays, suggestive conversation, ogling eyes, caresses, loving embraces, handling of one's own or another's body, passionate kisses, etc., will ordinarily cause the beginnings of venereal pleasure.

Since this reaction is automatic, the only way to control it is to cut off its source. No individual can validly protest that he "does not want the pleasure," if without any reason he continues the act which directly brings it on. He cannot will the cause and protest the effect.[1] Therefore, imagination, touch, sight, hearing, or anything potentially immodest must be controlled. Children should first be taught to control (not suppress!) their imagination. Then they should absorb a spontaneous modesty in dress and action. As they grow older, they should learn the connection of immodest acts with the danger of arousing passion. In this way they will acquire that enlightened self-control which purity presupposes.

How To Control the Imagination

It is not enough to say to a child, "Now, you ought to control your imagination." The child must be shown how. Images cannot be *forced* from the mind. Such an attempt will but fix the image more firmly. As an example, imagine a beautiful diamond ring before your eyes. Now keep saying, "I do not want to think of a diamond ring. Ring, away from my mind!" Do you see how the ring remains central in your effort? To eliminate the picture of the ring, you might concentrate on a golden orchid to harmonize with your mauve dress

---

1. For exceptions and conditions, cf. Principles III and IV in the Moral Section, Chapter VIII.

(or, if you are a man, imagine a pin-stripe double-breasted blue suit). The ring is gone. Only by substituting a vivid and detailed image of something equally, or more, attractive can an undesirable image be changed. Therefore, to help change an image, remember this motto: "Details carve an image." When we tell a child to think of something else, we speak wisely; but "something else" is too vague. The best way to introduce a new image is by minute visualization, the more detailed the better. No one who likes a "banana split" can have an immodest image in his mind if he can see his favorite confection down to the brown dots on the bananas! Since all children and adolescents are skilled (though they may not admit it) at make-believe, give them a definite subject of equal or greater attraction and the disturbing images will disappear.

Opportunities for teaching imagination control can be found in nightmare and "can't sleep" difficulties by showing the child how to go off to sleep thinking of something else. First, wake the child completely (for if he is only half awake, his mental slant will return him to the same dream); then suggest a topic for make-believe or imagination control: "Remember that trip we made to New York last year? Remember how you liked that ferry ride? What did you like about it? Now go off to sleep planning how you would use that ferry just for yourself!" A picnic trip, amusement park, window-shopping jaunt, can all be used. In a similar way, help him when he discovers difficulty with study, distractions in prayer, etc. Here, of course, the imagination should be stimulated in the direction of an activity rather than away from it.

Some young people have special images upon which they call in times of temptation: planning of a model airplane, boatbuilding, dressmaking, devising electrical contraptions or photographic equipment, etc. Some play out mentally a game of ball, tennis or chess. It is, then, easy to see the advantage of an absorbing hobby. There is a similar advantage in games and toys which demand ingenuity. As a matter of fact, we do too much for children, for modern toys are over-perfect mechanically, and even childhood games are now cut and dried. Few, if any of them, leave room for inventiveness. Modern recreation for adolescents too frequently fails in this respect. Too many young people today listen to TV, the radio, watch movies or ball games, and go places to *be* entertained. They do not know how to be active. Sports or other interests should be encouraged in which they can be moderately successful and which demand effort of body and mind, such as tennis, swimming, volley ball, baseball, football, basketball, ping-pong, badminton, boxing, music, hiking, skiing—in short, anything in which they can become engrossed bodily, mentally and imaginatively.

We should like to point out here the need not only for hobbies but also for truly intellectual pursuits which are not mere side lines. Modern American culture tends to regard the day's work, whether supporting a family or going to school, as time lost from more worthwhile pursuits, which to many are recreation and hobbies. Yet each one's daily work, no matter how humble, should be engrossing and interesting. It will become interesting when one sees it as a whole without excessive concentration on the trials and difficulties. In the same way, school work should be interesting for children, and parents should encourage this interest. If a young person really enjoyed the study of religion, history, sociology, good literature, languages, sciences, psychology or mathematics (all of which could be enjoyable were adults ready to provide an encouraging background), that youth would have little time or inclination for forbidden romancings, and would hardly ever choose sexual topics to fill the silences in social meetings. Indeed, there would be no silences! In struggling to encourage intellectual and cultural pursuits, parents may seem to wage an ever-losing battle with their environment; yet the slightest gain will bear fruit in happiness and contentment for their children.

Venereal Motions and Physical Condition

Sexual feeling is liable to arise, even spontaneously, if the general physical condition is either very high or very low. If one is fresh, pleasantly relaxed, full of vitality, and has nothing to do, or, on the other hand, is markedly weary or even exhausted, sexual motion may arise unbidden. Consequently, moderation is demanded in the activities of the young. As a general rule, children should be reasonably tired at bedtime from a busy interesting day, not from sheer boredom. Adolescents, too, should be busy but not dropping from exhaustion. For these and other reasons, late hours should be forbidden. Every adolescent needs at least eight hours of sleep and should have them.

Moderation in cleanliness, luxury, etc., is also important. Beds should not be too soft, nor covering too warm. Clothing should not be too tight or caressing, food too rich, furniture too luxurious, baths too hot. Again, a dirty, sticky body may lead to temptation, while on the other hand a fanatically well-cared-for body, effeminately clean, may likewise be a danger. In these as in most other things, a common-sense, middle course is best.

It happens, though rarely, that a child experiences almost continual sexual reactions through no fault of his own. In such a case, the help of a competent physician should be sought immediately, since the condition probably has a physical cause which can be corrected.

When unbidden physical temptation arises, forcible attempts to conquer it will rarely be successful. Rather, teach the child to change position, loosen tight clothing, go for a brisk walk, etc. Thus, natural energy will be directed into proper healthy channels and drained from this sexual preoccupation.

Cycle of Temptation

Whether the devil is responsible, or whether the fact is founded in our human nature, there seems to be a cycle or rhythm in temptations. For several weeks they may come in avalanches. Then, for a week or two, there will be comparative quiet. We think the battle is over, and sigh with relief. But no! The devil seems to leave off in this way just so we will drop our defenses and be caught by the next barrage. After the lull comes a fresh storm. We see from this that vigilance, prayer, and caution about the occasions of sin should continue. In time of peace, prepare for war! If prayer and alertness are steadily maintained, the temptations will gradually be conquered. But if, in times of quiet, chances are taken with dangerous reading, etc., when the temptation returns, its force may be too great for us.

PSYCHOLOGY OF BOYS AND GIRLS

Boys are more tempted to physical pleasure (in imagination and reality), whereas girls are rather attracted to the romantic. Boys naturally tend to be active, to look, to caress, to take the initiative. Girls are naturally receptive. They desire *to be* attractive, to draw loving glances and attention, *to be* embraced, etc. A knowledge of this difference of reaction in the sexes is of great importance for adolescents. Boys must learn to guard their eyes, to control their active tendencies, to beware of familiarities, to restrain their bent to quick sexual excitement. Girls should avoid daring dress, excessively romantic love stories, the use of wrong means to gain attention, and they should restrain their desire for caresses.

On dates, each partner should feel responsible for the other. A caress that would be carelessly welcomed by a girl is likely to kindle a fire of passion in the boy. She should understand this; and also, she should know that once her passions are aroused she may possibly have less control than the boy. On the other hand, the boy should understand that a girl's welcome reception of a caress or embrace does not necessarily indicate desire for sexual pleasure on her part. It is true that responsibility for sins on dates is usually about equal, for the boy should have restrained his active tendencies and the girl her passive ones. Yet, because of her slower reactions which provide time for weighing the consequences of her acts, a girl will find that she can be in command of any situation, provided she has chosen a reasonably upright boy for her partner. The members of each sex will find that, although different things must be guarded against by each, the necessary quantity of restraint, self-control and mortification is about equal for both.

Understanding this difference of masculine and feminine reactions will be of value to young people when they enter marriage. The masculine nature seeks quick physical satisfaction, the feminine nature demands prolonged marks and expressions of love. The very knowledge they have used to prevent sin before marriage, can be rightly used to help express their love in marriage.

PSYCHOLOGY OF STIMULATION

It is necessary to dwell for a moment on the various kinds of immodesty which are to be seen on all sides. Examples include pin-ups, "cheesecake" and "billboard art," excessively scanty swimming, dancing or sport costumes. These kinds of immodesty are found both in real life and in pictures, whether drawn, painted, photographed or moving.[2] There is no doubt that adolescents find this fashion of nudity or nearnudity a great source of conflict. Their Catholic instinct and training warn them of the danger of such cos-

---

2. Immodesty of dress may mean other things besides scantiness of attire. Clothing which covers the body adequately may be immodest if its design draws attention to certain parts of the body, or if it is very tight.

tumes, and yet it is difficult to act against the pagan manners of the times. It is a great help to them to have practiced modesty from an early age, and it is also helpful for them to understand why these immodesties are wrong.

First of all, it is hardly deniable that the sight of the female breast and thigh, whether in reality or pictured, is sexually stimulating to the ordinary male. The stimulation is greater if these parts of the body are lightly veiled, artistically accentuated, or if the clothing seems about to fall off. "Art" can hardly be urged as a justification, because many editors, columnists, story writers, and night-club owners frankly admit this appeal to the lower passions.[3] Some authorities hold this body worship responsible for many marital difficulties and even for marital infidelity. Now, if this costuming or lack of it is sexually stimulating, it is more or less sinful to indulge in it; that is, generally speaking, it is more or less sinful to look at such pictures or appear in such costumes, depending on the circumstances (cf. Moral Principles III and IV).

However, it is sometimes difficult to understand why these things are sexually stimulating. If the body is good, why must we hide it in clothing? It might seem that, as long as the sexual organs themselves are covered, further precautions are unnecessary. The answer is this: Sexual stimulation involves more than the sexual organs themselves. Certain bodily zones are involved in the acts preliminary to a marriage embrace. The male is naturally attracted to see and touch these regions. The female is naturally attracted to be seen and touched. Living as they do in the midst of what may be called a cult of nudity, adolescents (particularly girls) do not realize the sexual implications of this undress. For their own good, therefore, it is necessary to make them understand it.

---

3. Cf. "The Picture Magazines," in *Harper's*, July, 1943, pp. 159ff.; "Footnote on Sex," in *Harper's*, March, 1946, pp. 212ff.; "So This Is Cheesecake," in *Popular Photography*, February, 1946, pp. 34ff.; "Is It Anyone We Know?" in *Harper's*, June, 1946, pp. 496ff.

Lifelong training in a reasonable and reasoned modesty of eyes, touch, and dress is necessary for all. For the young child, modesty of dress should mean remaining covered at all times except in necessity, for example, at bath times, sickness, inspection by parents, etc. Modesty of eyes should mean not inspecting the bodies of others. Modesty of touch should mean "hands off" the private parts of self or others. At first, the reason for these practices can be based on desire for one's own privacy and respect for the privacy of others. Later the Third and Fourth Moral Principles can be given in a general way; that is, it is forbidden to chance sexual stimulation in oneself or another without some good and sufficient reason. Finally, if and when an adolescent refuses to recognize the danger to himself or another (the latter is sometimes more difficult to see), parents must indicate the reason behind training in modesty. "These attractive parts of the body are used in the preliminaries of the marriage act (or, the act from which children come). Since you are not married, you have no right to either the marriage act or to the preliminaries. So be sensible, guard your eyes, refuse to follow the fashion of nudity, of petting, passionate kissing, etc., for all these things have the same reasons against them."

Movies cause difficulty not only by setting up models of immodest dress, but also by portraying the passionate kiss. Usually this portrayal is not too dangerous to view as long as the onlookers do not identify themselves with the actors. However, what is seen on the screen is often imitated in real life. Many teen-agers try out the "technique" learned from the screen on their next date. Then, of course, their purity is endangered.[4]

---

4. Cf. Fleege, *op. cit.*, pp. 250-258.

PSYCHOLOGY OF LOVE

Even among Catholics, the most amazing ideas of love's true nature exist. Some think that love is automatic and inevitable. In their opinion, once a person "falls in love," nothing can be done about it. Should a non-Catholic, or a divorced person, or a drunkard be the object of that love, it was nevertheless so destined. For such people, love is caught like a contagious disease. Similarly, many think that once love is felt, any expression of it, whether moral or not, is perfectly legitimate.[5] People very commonly hold these opinions because they identify romantic love with all love. Though they speak of parental love and divine love, few consider these "real love" since the romantic element is lacking.

Love can exist on the level of reason and will, the emotional or romantic level, and the physical level or that of sexual passion. Conjugal love should comprise all three levels in a combination which may vary from couple to couple and from circumstance to circumstance. However, in its simplest sense, love is merely the desire of something good. When a person desires something good for himself, he loves with the love of concupiscence, a love which can easily degenerate into greedy selfishness. When he desires that good for someone else, he loves with the love of benevolence, a more noble well-wishing purified of all self-interest. It should be obvious that marriage must rest on a mutual love of well-wishing. Marriage experts all agree that selfishness is the greatest enemy of happiness in marriage.[6]

Now, strong emotional or romantic feelings may accompany either the love of concupiscence or the love of benevolence; just as physical passion can accompany either. *But neither the romantic feelings nor the passion must be considered the basis of true love.*

Why? First of all, when emotion or passion is made

5. *Cf. ibid.,* p. 294.
6. Cf. Mace, David, *Marriage Counseling* (J. A. Churchill, London, 1948), pp. 117-118.

the desired good, love soon fades, because neither emotion nor passion is under complete control of the lovers. When emotion and passion die, and die they will from time to time as their object becomes an accustomed one, there is nothing else to love! And secondly, love based only on emotion and passion is naturally selfish because the thrill of emotion or the sexual pleasure is the object of desire. The lover naturally wants it for himself, and it is extremely difficult to desire these thrills for his beloved *unless he loves for some other reason!* On what, then, can true love be based? It can be based only on the real or potential qualities of the beloved *person.* Once a lover recognizes his beloved as a person who is agreeable, lovable, full of good qualities with more to be developed; once the lover is willing to sacrifice himself, to give *all* of himself to the beloved, then and then only can he claim to love with nobility. When his main concern is the entire good of his beloved (both spiritual and physical), then romance and physical desire may (and should) embroider and complete the love.

The emergence of the love upon which marriage may safely be based, does not follow any set pattern. In some cases, romance or physical desire may precede *love of a person.* Occasionally physical desire is long delayed. Whatever the pattern for rising love, it is always important that the mind guide the heart, that reason guide the will, that clear vision guide the feelings. Hence it is imperative to caution the adolescent lest he identify his love of romance with love of the person who may cause the romantic feelings. A bobby-soxer's swoon at the sight of a curly head or the sound of a husky voice is not love.[7]

---

7. For a further analysis of the nature of love, cf. Farrell, Walter, O. P., *A Companion to the Summa* (Sheed and Ward, New York, 1940), Vol. III, pp. 61ff.

In Love with Love

In this connection, St. Augustine offers a penetrating analysis which may help to explain some thoughtless sins.[8] Young people feel very much the need of love even before realizing what it really is. They are "in love with love." They are so anxious to experience this adult emotion that they often try out whatever popular opinion considers it to be: if it is sexual liberty, petting or kissing, then they experiment with these means in the attempt to discover this thing that everyone talks about. Occasionally they go even further, despite their better judgment, simply under the force of romantic propaganda. The results are of course as ashes in their mouths, for physical love can only bring real joy when subordinated to higher spiritual values, and when used according to God's law, in marriage. Natural law and moral law both come from God; they cannot be in opposition to each other.

Young men and women must understand that there is sufficient time to discover the fullness of conjugal love in marriage, and that they will but blunt this holy love if they try to find it too soon. The time of adolescence is the time to grow up. The happy experiences of meeting other boys and girls, and of learning the arts of social life, must not be sacrificed to an eagerness for present enjoyment of every possible thrill.

Attraction

There are several steps of attraction between the sexes, all of them on the emotional level. They are, a *general attraction* to the other sex, a *particular attraction* to an individual, and lastly, a *physical attraction*.

On reaching puberty, boys and girls are surprised and sometimes alarmed to find themselves attracted to each other whereas a few months before they were repelled. Girls realize with amazement that they are

8. Cf. *op. cit.*, Book 3, chapter 1, p. 41.

attracted to *older* boys, and that they themselves feel shy and afraid! Explain to girls that they mature earlier (though boys catch up later); and also that their shyness is due to discomfort in a new situation and to a natural modesty which urges caution. Neither boys nor girls should be teased concerning this new awareness, nor, on the other hand, treated with all sorts of solemn warnings. It is best to show that this change is perfectly natural. Kindly fun in the family circle is permissible as long as it does not degenerate into the sort of joking that is very hard on its victim. Any fun-making should involve and express pride that a son or daughter is growing up. If warnings are necessary, always add that the attraction to the opposite sex is natural at their age and to be expected. From this time on, meetings of adolescents for outings and fun together should be not so much hindered as supervised.

Attraction to a particular person will then follow. Personal attraction is usually felt for someone who complements a boy or girl emotionally and intellectually. The two "get along" together. This emotional, personal attraction may grow to the proportions of a "puppy love" affair. A first crush of this kind should usually be ignored. The youth will grow out of it rather quickly. Only if the person involved is of dubious character should steps be taken—and then with the greatest delicacy, for the adolescent may resent interference. At a later date, such an emotional or romantic attachment will be a prelude to marriage. Even in that case, the attachment must be guided by intellect and will. If the person who is the object of such emotion is of poor character or marriage is impossible for a long time to come, the individual must "fall out of love." Should the romance continue without any possibility of marriage, it will almost certainly lead to sin. The remedy is the usual one of removing the cause: not seeing the person, getting rid of keepsakes, pictures, etc., and busying the mind about other things. Generally speaking, it *is* possible to "fall out of love" even when romantic attachment is involved.

Physical or venereal attraction may come at any time, *with or without love or romantic attraction.* It has its proper place in marriage, but unfortunately does not always stay there. Both the married and the unmarried must be careful of physical attraction to others.[9]

PSYCHOLOGY OF DISCIPLINE

Discipline is most difficult to describe. It is the training of the character of a child. The objective of discipline is to develop the child's moral fiber so that he can gradually stand alone as an integrated personality with all his appetites and desires under proper control. Discipline is *interior* and *exterior.* Interior discipline is simply self-control which keeps all activity directed to the goal of life. Exterior discipline means the external controls which gradually bring about interior discipline.

To form interior discipline or self-control, it is necessary to give the child the best of good example and all possible good motives, natural and supernatural—from the motive of becoming mature to that of acting for love of God. For example, a child should learn control of his tendency to blurt out all the family secrets. This he can do only if he has the example of his parents who keep *his* little secrets. Further, he needs the motives of loyalty to family; of desire to be sufficiently "grown-up" to be trusted with a secret; and ultimately, of loyalty to God.

For a child to absorb such high motives, however, takes time. Therefore, until such internal discipline is learned, parents must help along with exterior discipline: they must be good disciplinarians. This does not

---

9. For this whole section on attraction, falling in and out of love, etc., cf. Kelly, Gerald, S. J., *Modern Youth and Chastity* (The Queen's Work, St. Louis, 1941), pp. 14-28, 39-41.
Note: This was republished as *Chastity: A Guide for Teens and Young Adults* (Roman Catholic Books, P.O. Box 255, Harrison, NY 10528).—*Editor,* 1993.

mean to be strict and severe, as so many believe. "A good disciplinarian is one who can influence a group (or even one person) to keep themselves in order."[10]

How can parents influence their children to keep themselves in order? Besides good example and the constant inculcation of good motives, they must use the external helps of *reward* and *punishment*.

Reward

Many parents are afraid to use reward to teach virtue because they feel it is an attempt to *pay* a child for acting virtuously. This is a mistake. True, we should not attempt to pay for virtue, but payment and reward are quite distinct. Payment is giving an agreed amount for a proportionate effort. For example, some parents pay a child a certain sum of money weekly for washing dishes (most authorities are against such a practice). Reward, however, is not proportionate to the action (it may be greater or less), and it is not agreed upon beforehand. As an instance of the wise use of reward, consider this incident. A father noticed a torn-up comic book in his young son's wastebasket. When he questioned the youngster, he found that the booklet was discarded because the pictures were immodest. Very much impressed, the father immediately purchased a beautiful child's book which his son had long desired, as a palpable reward for the virtuous action.

Virtue is its own reward, in the sense that any really virtuous action is a perfection and when one is conscious of the perfection he feels bigger and more a man or woman. But children do not experience this so easily, and the difficulty of triumphing over their passions, such as anger or desire for fun, seems at times to outweigh the satisfaction of virtue. Hence, parents must implement the interior satisfaction with wise material rewards and also with *praise* and social approval or *honor.*

---

10. Copeland, Norman C., *Psychology of the Soldier* (Military Service Publishing Co., Harrisburg, 1942), p. 36. Quoted with permission of the publisher.

Honest praise is a powerful reward, which unfortunately is not used sufficiently by parents to encourage virtue. Too often we take goodness for granted and notice only the faults. A little girl had been trying to be good all day, and when it was time for bed, her mother found her in tears. When questioned, the tot replied: "Well, haven't I been *pretty* good today?" What a world of difference a few words of praise would have made!

Virtue does not receive, either in the family or in society at large, the honor which is its due. Our modern world honors power and success, but gives little recognition to honesty, purity and modesty. How much easier it would be for us if we were to give our youth real models of purity and modesty, by granting honor to those who practice real virtue.

It is difficult, if not impossible, to praise *purity* in a child, simply because purity is non-activity so far as observable phenomena are concerned. But certainly the praise of pure persons in history and among the child's list of acquaintances can be used to insinuate good habits into a child's soul. Praise is more effective in the realm of modesty, which is observable. If we praise the child for modesty of eyes, of dress, of choice of entertainment, a great deal of real self-control will ensue. For example, to praise a girl for the wise choice of a modest yet attractive dress, or a boy for his careful check of the Legion of Decency ratings before going to a movie, will greatly increase the practice of modesty. Luckily, honor is gradually being given to attractive modesty. Teen-age girls and boys are joining a Sodality program called the Fighting Sixty-ninth (for the Sixth and Ninth Commandments). This program gives social approval to modesty of costume, and indeed brings social pressures to bear. The program has a slogan— SDS—Supply the Demand for the Supply. Once fashion designers found a demand for modest clothing, a demand the teen-agers themselves supplied through their own fashion shows, they were quite willing to meet the market with suitable clothing.

Rewards are an extremely powerful added incentive to purity and modesty, and parents will do well to use sensible material rewards, and also sincere praise and honor, to help the growth of their children in virtue.

Punishment

St. Thomas indicates three reasons for punishment.[11] The first reason uses punishment to prevent an individual from harming himself, even though he does not, or cannot, recognize the danger. Thus, we punish a baby when he reaches for the fire or a hot stove, toaster, etc., to deter him from doing what will hurt him. In the same way, we might slap the hands of a child who plays with his genitals lest he develop a dangerous habit. However, such punishment should not be severe or "adult size." If it is naughty for a child to suck his thumb, it is naughty to play with these organs, and no more so.

Secondly, punishment is used to induce correct action through fear, so that a good habit is formed. Once this is done, the good reasons behind the action can gradually be substituted as a motive instead of the fear. This of course demands that the reasons for the good action be explained. How often we all have learned in this way! Recall the wholesome punishment you received for disobedience, sauciness, lying, etc., which helped you learn obedience, truthfulness, respect, and all that you knew was right and just. This kind of punishment, *with reasons,* should be given for immodesty, or any dangerous action which might involve someone else. For example, a youngster of 7 who disobeys your command to remain covered, should be punished. He will learn the habit of modesty even though he will only later fully understand the reasons.

Retribution is the third reason for punishment. Strict

---

11. *Summa Theologica,* II-II, q. 108, a. 4.

justice demands that every sin or crime be matched with the precise amount of punishment due, either in this life or in the next. Now, perfect justice will be administered in the next life by God's judgment. In this life we cannot, and indeed should not, try to match every fault with the exact measure of punishment due for it. Should we attempt such strict justice, we would be liable to excessive severity and rigidity. Justice tempered with mercy must be the norm here below.

Nevertheless, a fault cannot be ignored. A child's own good demands that almost every fault bring some punishment. We cannot let him "get away with it" because he must learn that crime does not pay, even in this life. This reason for punishment should be used, for example, when a child realizes his fault and is sorry, and yet needs some corrective measure to impress the matter on his mind. Some penalty should be imposed, though it may be lightened or even lifted after a brief time. This is the kind of punishment which properly fits the attitude of "this hurts me more than it hurts you."

Punishment must be *consistent.* If children are punished for one act and unpunished (or worse, smilingly indulged!) for another of the same kind, they make no progress in judging right from wrong. The younger the child, the more *swift, immediate,* and *brief* should be the punishment. A young child's mind will find no connection between the fault and a punishment given long afterward, and he will be bewildered, not helped. Since the young child lives almost wholly in the present moment, a long punishment will seem like a lifetime. As the child grows into puberty and adolescence, slower, more remote, or longer punishments may be given, indicating that the parent has considered the matter and calmly judged it as it is. Such deliberation will also indicate that the axe inevitably falls sooner or later for wrongdoing.

Punishment and the Sixth Commandment

All three reasons for punishment may be used for external faults against purity or modesty, but overly harsh punishments are out of order for several reasons. First, undue attention may be drawn to these matters long before a child is able to understand the nature of his "crime." As an example, were a child of 7 to be violently spanked in horrified anger at some childish indecency, his mind might be "fixed" in tremendous fear on a matter he does not fully understand. Try always to match the punishment to his understanding and guilt. Secondly, overly harsh punishments might drive the sin underground. Since impurity can be such an individual and personal thing, severe punishment might merely force the sin from an open position where it could be corrected to a hidden level where you will never discover it.

Two cautions are imperative. *Rarely if ever should physical punishment be used for personal impurity* (masturbation, or any of the individual acts listed under the First Moral Principle). In the child's mind, physical punishment might become associated with the impurity and the association could perhaps grow into some perversion. Secondly, *never send a child to bed for a fault of this kind.* To do this might be to send him right into the sin you are trying to correct, because he is not tired and has nothing to occupy his mind except his crime and its punishment. This would certainly be dangerous. Correct the child, punish him with deprivations if you think it prudent; but above all be sympathetic, pointing out the spiritual and natural reasons for purity and also the helps necessary to attain it.

PSYCHOLOGY OF ADOLESCENCE

We cannot attempt in these few pages to give you the whole adolescent psychology. Even the specialists are not too certain of their position and much research is still needed.[12] However, a few important statements about sexual troubles in adolescence must be made.

First, sexual development is by no means the *lone* problem of adolescence, nor is it, in itself, the *chief* problem. If it were the only problem, it would be relatively easy to handle. It looms so large because of the continual stress laid upon it in popular literature and because the adolescent himself, in trying to cope with the problems of his development, tends to fasten his mind on his rapidly changing body as the source of his difficulties. Frequently, however, sexual imaginings and even masturbation are *symptoms* of other problems rather than problems in themselves. When this is the case we waste time and energy (to say nothing of doing positive harm) if we treat the symptom and do not find the disorder. Moral warnings and instruction are necessary, but they are not the only remedies to be applied.

Growing up to be a mature adult is the chief problem of adolescence, for adolescence is a time of in-between. The individual feels he is no longer a child, and yet he is not grown up. He wants to take his place among adults and yet feels inadequate to the task. He is attempting to push away all parental props, to take his first steps alone and unaided; and at the same time he feels the need of his parents more than ever. He is beginning to look around and see the world and its problems for the first time. Getting along in a social world has taken on new importance, and many a youngster wonders whether he is secure in the esteem of his friends or even of his parents. Occasionally, a sexual experiment at this age is really an attempt to prove "maturity" to himself or others. It results from fear of being "just a kid."

Adjustment to the fresh, bewildering, turbulent, changing reality of the world is made even more dif-

---

12. We urge those who are interested in this subject to read: Schneiders, Alexander A., *Personality Development and Adjustment in Adolescence* (Bruce, Milwaukee, 1960).

ficult by the fact that the adolescent himself is changing rapidly.

Not only does the world about him seem to change every day, but his point of view is changing as fast. His body alters and grows rapidly. He hasn't the muscular coordination he had a short time before. He is suddenly clumsy. His emotional capacity is growing along with his ability to grasp and penetrate the meaning of things. He hardly wakes on two consecutive days feeling he is the same individual. Picture someone trying to keep his balance in a room when the walls and floors are moving, while his legs have lost their responsiveness to his brain. This gives a fair image of the plight of the adolescent, who cannot feel confident of either the world around him or himself.

Though this is a difficult time (which we all have experienced, even if we have since forgotten it), it is not so bad *if there is a chance of successful adjustment.* Here is where parents count. A word of honest praise now and then, with less criticism and faultfinding, will help. A boy or girl who finds every effort regarded as clumsy, silly, foolish, and far short of the mark, soon gets discouraged, gives up the attempt, and takes refuge in daydreams. Lessen your demands for a while. Instead of expecting a top scholastic record, be satisfied and appreciative if only a few points are gained. Instead of demanding perfect behavior and manners, show appreciation of an honest effort in the right direction, even though you make it clear that there is more to be done. Never, at this time, let a desired perfection be the enemy of even a slight actual advance.

Daydreams

Daydreams are part of adolescent growth, and yet they can be very dangerous. If daydreams are an approach to *real plans* for the future, they are a part of the healthy romanticism of youth, and hence are good. A boy who dreams of the day when he will be a priest, a lawyer, a builder, the father of a family—a boy who makes resolutions and plans and tries to put them into practice—is using his dreams profitably, though he will hardly reach the heights of success of which he dreams. This holds also for a girl who dreams of the sisterhood, of motherhood, nursing, and a hundred other careers or triumphs. If, however, the daydreams are wild and built of stuff far too thin for reality, they are a real peril. The dream which puts the dreamer on a pedestal with all the world in adulation at his feet, is unhealthy. It is merely a refuge from the reality which the adolescent has failed to meet. Here is the norm: *If a dream has a connection with a reasonable possibility, it is good; if it is outside the realm of possibility, it is dangerous.* If a boy of good athletic ability dreams of being a Big League Pitcher, his dream will do no harm even though he ends up still an amateur. But if his dreams are of himself as an ambidextrous pitcher who cannot lose a game, or a home run specialist who bats 1.000 his first season, his dream is unhealthy. (Don't laugh; this is a daydream in which a boy of poor athletic ability actually indulged!)

Dangerous as the wild daydream is in itself, there is a greater danger involved: that it will wander into the field of romantic love. This holds particularly for girls, though it is true of both sexes. Such romantic daydreams may degenerate into imaginings of sexual triumph and the wildest obscenities. They may even lead to masturbation.

Sexual imaginations and sexual excesses may, therefore, have either of two causes. First, they may be sought for themselves; that is, simply for the pleasure involved. This problem can be attacked directly: by explaining what is wrong in such daydreams and actions, by making clear the challenge to self-control, and by urging the religious helps, as indicated above.

The second reason is the impulse to take refuge from reality. An adolescent may indulge in sexuality and evil imaginings, not for themselves (indeed, often with distaste), but because these things give him a dream-world in which he cannot be a failure. This must be met indirectly, by making sure the adolescent knows he is loved and appreciated at home and among his friends. To *tell* this to an adolescent is not sufficient, he must *experience* it. He must be shown.

The adolescent attempting to build an adult personality will, of course, scarcely ever indicate the precise nature of his imaginings. To do so would be to lose what little self-respect they have given him. The most that parents can do is to try, without prying, to understand the youngster's problem. A parent must be willing to help or to stand on the side lines till needed. Try to keep the 13-to-17-year-olds occupied. Prevent their mooning about and daydreaming, but do this indirectly because scolding will not help. Be cautious of stressing the note of blame, and search for acts you can genuinely praise. If a problem of personal sexuality (masturbation or obscene imagination) is brought to you, use both the above methods. Indicate the sin, why it is wrong, and the methods of overcoming it. Then point out that daydreaming is harmful because it is a flight from reality. Urge the boy or girl to possible, or probable, successful efforts. Finally, make sure that they are successful in *something!* They need only a firm place to anchor their maturing personalities. Try to provide it.

We admit that our sketch of the teen years is very inclusively drawn. Few adolescents go through every stage of the complete turmoil we have described. Yet all adolescents have *some* of the difficulties enumerated, to a greater or lesser degree. We merely point these things out so that you will have some understanding of them. Frequently an adolescent will go through these stages without help, and will hardly remember them later.[13]

---

13. To appreciate these difficulties as they affect boys, consult Fleege, *op. cit.*, chapters 16 and 17.

QUESTIONS AND DISCUSSION AIDS

1. How does passion rise? Is its origin the same for each sex? Is it directly under control of the will? How can it be controlled? How can one change an image? Discuss some methods you have used in this or other fields.

2. What is wrong with passive recreation? (*It calls into activity little if any vital power.*) What is the value of hobbies, intellectual pursuits, etc.?

3. Has physical condition anything to do with venereal pleasure? What is a good position on the subject of bodily cleanliness?

4. Have you experienced cyclic temptations in this or other spheres? Does our explanation help? Do you think it would help boys and girls? What is the difference between sexual reaction in boys and girls? How can this knowledge help them?

5. What is wrong with semi-nudity on stage, screen, in magazine pictures, etc.? Does it give any sexual information? Can *you* do anything to correct these evils alone? With others?

6. What is love? Is physical or romantic attraction necessary for it? Does modern literature think so? Is it true that youth is "in love with love"?

7. Did you ever realize that there are three kinds of attraction between the sexes? Does this knowledge present some worries about your children? Should it?

8. Discuss ways and means of using reward, praise and honor to inculcate purity and modesty. What is your reaction to this book's analysis of punishment? Are you of the opinion that punishment is outmoded as an educational force? Do you believe in frequent corporal punishment? Moderate? None at all? Why?

9. Joe, a boy of 16, went with a group to a girl's house. He arrived home at three A. M. Confronted by his anxious parents, he admitted that the gang had left at eleven and he had stayed on *alone* until the young lady's parents returned from a trip. When his mother protested

on grounds of propriety, he retorted, "Oh, you have an evil mind." His angry father immediately punished him by confiscating a new rifle, his choicest possession. Both parents mentioned the incident to Joe's married brothers and sisters, each of whom took him aside to talk things over. Analyze this case from the point of view of punishment. Granted he committed no sins of impurity or immodesty, should he have felt some doubts about such a situation? Did he have any obligation to this girl's reputation? Does original sin have any place in the discussion? At his age, should he have known better, aside from specific warnings from his parents? Was the punishment too severe? Granted he did not think his action wrong, should he have been punished anyhow?

10. Is your justice toward your children mixed with mercy? Are your actions consistent? Is physical punishment useful in curbing impurity? Immodesty?

11. Is the chief problem of adolescence the sexual one? Should adolescence be the time for a special campaign on chastity? Must sexual troubles, temptations, etc., always be treated directly?

12. Despite their tendency to keep to themselves, do you think adolescents will accept help?[14]

13. Is there any danger in daydreams? In what kind?

14. Propose some methods of giving security to an adolescent without being false to yourself and to the child (that is, methods of praising where praise is due, without lowering reasonable standards). Discuss them.

---

14. Cf. *ibid.*, pp. 62-90.

Chapter XI

Physiological Content Of Catholic Sex Education

When one picks up a modern non-Catholic pamphlet on sex education, one becomes concerned at the greatly detailed physiological instruction. One such text, for example,[1] is supposedly written to be given piecemeal to a child from his earliest years until about 8. In it, the young child learns the words: egg, ovary, embryo, placenta, sperm, penis, scrotum, vulva, uterus, breasts, nipples, fetus, navel. He learns also the process of birth and the precise nature of sexual intercourse, and is exposed to a rather complete diagram of female sexual anatomy.

One wonders why all this detail is necessary. Many intelligent grown-ups would be unable to identify all these terms, and still they manage to live reasonably complete lives. It seems senseless to preoccupy a child with all this information at such an early age. We do not see the same space and terminology given to the explanation of digestion, hearing, sight, walking, or any other bodily function. Yet everyone is expected to use these various faculties and to control them according to the moral law. Besides all this, such emphasis on any bodily function is unhealthy. Hypochondriacs are born of an excessive consciousness of the heart, stomach, muscles, etc. When such attention is given to a

---

1. Faegre, Marion L., *Your Own Story,* University of Minnesota Press, Minneapolis, 1943.

function which is excessively attractive to the passions, it is even worse. Therefore, let us have a great deal of discretion in discussing this matter of anatomy and physiology.[2]

Many modern authors on these subjects advance two reasons for their insistence on detailed technical information. First, they seem convinced that technical terminology will obviate most emotional urges. Secondly, they think that an early and complete knowledge of sex will prevent unwholesome curiosity, and will of itself engender the virtue of chastity. Each of these reasons embodies some truth, but they are not completely valid as they stand.

Technical terms may indeed *help* to prevent emotion in discussion simply because they do not so easily bring up the corresponding mental images; for example, if we speak of the duodenum, we can easily discuss the intestine without imagining it pictorially. In sexual matters, correct terms have further value because the only other words are either vulgar, obscene or childish. If the vulgar terms are used, images and evil thoughts are liable to follow. If the childish terms are used, adults or adolescents will be embarrassed at the limitation of their vocabulary when precise reference is needed later. Nevertheless, technical words do not, of themselves, *prevent* sexual passion or evil thoughts and desires. Sin may be committed with technical as well as with non-technical knowledge, for images may be called up even by the technical terms, and sinful action may accompany scientific knowledge.

Curiosity is, indeed, somewhat allayed by scientific terms and a reasonable knowledge imparted in due time. A girl who is instructed in the sixth grade in a general way about the origin of life will consider the first conversations she hears from her companions "old stuff." She will also realize immediately some of the false ideas they have because she knows she has been

2. Cf. Cabot, Richard, M. D., *Christianity and Sex,* Macmillan, New York, 1938.

given it "straight" by her parents and can obtain more information when she asks. The mystery is to a large extent gone. Yet this knowledge will hardly prevent her reading or re-reading a "doctor's book" if one is at hand, simply because curiosity in matters of sex is never completely satisfied. Nor will curiosity of the eyes be satisfied by mere knowledge of sexual organs. If it were, "sexy" advertisements would have long since disappeared, because one illustration tells as much as a hundred. Lastly, virtue is not created by knowledge, simply because virtue is not a matter of mind but of will. Knowledge of sexual apparatus may help in understanding the matters with which chastity is concerned, and in realizing why the virtue is important; but to build that virtue, the exercise of the will is needed.

Should Children Learn the Correct Names?

Admitting that the arguments just given have only partial value, it seems better nevertheless to teach the child the correct names from the beginning in so far as names are necessary. These words are no more difficult for him than "spinach" or "asparagus," and there is an advantage in the child's becoming familiar with them before he can associate them with an emotion or passion. They enable him to express his needs to a doctor, parent, nurse or priest, simply and correctly from the start. Many adults are still at a loss for words when consulting a doctor because they do not know the words, or if they know them, have not learned to use them without embarrassment. Yet how much more embarrassing are their substitutes!

For all these reasons we think every male child should know: penis, scrotum, buttocks, navel, anus, urine, urinate, bowels, and bowel movement. Every female child should know: vulva, breasts, and the rest as above beginning with buttocks. If there is any necessity to speak of the sexual organs of the other sex, then the correct terms (penis, scrotum; vulva, breasts) should be used. We do not say that all the sexual knowledge connected with these terms should be given, but only that if there is any need to refer to the organs the correct terms may be used from the beginning. This is quite different from that strictly sexual education described on the preceding page.

However, some people may feel uncomfortable and even ashamed to use this technical language. Some may even find it impossible. This is so true that we fear many a parent will say: "I cannot use such words with my children; I will not attempt it. Therefore, someone else must educate my children in sexual matters." For this reason we insist that terminology is not absolutely necessary. Use any words you find natural —nursery terms, or even "home-made" words—so long as you give your children the basic information and train them in virtue. The norm, then, is this: If you are a person who can easily use "navel" instead of "belly-button," then try to use the terms listed above; if you find the second word easier—then use any terms at all, for you must remember that words are but instruments of meaning. Precise terminology is only incidental to good sex education.

How Much Should Be Known?

Even for the married or about-to-be-married, a doctor's physiological knowledge is never really *necessary*. It may be *useful* and *interesting* for highly educated young people or married persons, but can be dispensed with even by them. Do you know what the epididymis, is, or the Graafian follicle? If you do, does it make much difference in your grappling with real life? Yet, these terms appear in many sex education booklets by non-Catholics even for children and adolescents!

Physiology Courses

There is no objection to courses in physiology which include the physiology of sexual functions, in the last year of high school, as long as they give no more emphasis to sexual organs than they give to other parts of the body. (Such a course should, however, be given separately to boys and girls.) Our reason for this position is that physiology is an accepted branch of human knowledge for that age. To omit the physiology of sexual organs from such a course might only draw unwholesome attention to them. Any dangers which might arise can be taken care of by due caution, an impersonal, objective, scientific approach and an application of the Third and Fourth Moral Principles in Chapter VIII. As is obvious, parents should not be expected to give children a formal course in physiology. Nor is there any need of a course of sexual physiology in grade school. Digestive, respiratory and sensitive functions are more than enough to keep young children busy and interested.

The following pages will attempt to give an outline: first, of the *maximum* information that, under any circumstances, parents can be expected to give their children; second, of the *minimum* that is needed for a reasonably complete sex education; and third, of the facts that are needed at various particular age levels. Before beginning it can be said that there is no particular value in anatomical charts for the education of children. Leave them to the medical or physiological classroom, for you certainly do not use charts for training in elimination, walking or speaking. Why use them here?

MAXIMUM MALE PHYSIOLOGY

The male organs of reproduction are mostly external. Two organs of the male are chiefly concerned in reproduction, the testicles or testes, and the penis. The testes are two small glands suspended in a sack (scrotum) from the trunk of the body between the thighs. They produce the sperm or seed which, when united to the egg produced in the organs of the female, develops into the body of a child. As the seed is produced, it is led through a number of canals or ducts and then stored until finally forcefully ejected (this is called ejaculation) through the penis. This happens in the marital act or during sleep. During sexual stimulation, the penis becomes erect and firm (this is called erection) for penetration into the vagina of the female where the seed is deposited. This act of penetration is called intercourse, coitus, coition, or the marital act. The penis is the chief source of sexual or venereal pleasure in the male. Any spontaneous movement or stiffening (erection) of this organ is usually an indication of the beginning of sexual pleasure and should be checked (except when properly to be used in marriage) by prayer, by exercise, by change of position, by diverting the mind, etc. Complete pleasure, with ejaculation of seed, is called orgasm. Deliberate orgasm is permissible only in a lawful marriage act. If intentional and alone, it is called self-satisfaction, self-abuse, pollution, or masturbation.

The loss of seed during the night without fault is called involuntary seminal emission, nocturnal pollution, loss of seed, or simply loss. This reaction merely expels the excess store of seed. Sexual dreams frequently, and quite naturally, accompany it, and an individual may recall that he brought it about by the use of his hands during sleep or the semi-conscious state before awakening fully. Nevertheless, neither reaction, dreams, nor the touches should cause the faintest disturbance if they are beyond the control of mind and will. If an adolescent wakens during the emission, though he should refuse voluntary delight in the pleasure and stop any action that may be causing it, he has no obligation of attempting to prevent the emission. Of course, to *cause* this emission by any means (self-abuse or masturbation) is sinful; but neither self-abuse nor nocturnal emission is a "loss of manhood" in any physical sense. Yet self-abuse is definitely a spiritual loss, in the sense of loss of manly self-control, and the loss of sanctifying grace by mortal sin.

MAXIMUM FEMALE PHYSIOLOGY

In the female, we may speak of internal and external sexual organs, though the truly reproductive organs are all internal. The external organs are the breasts and vulva. The internal are the ovaries, tubes, womb (or uterus), and vagina. The breasts after puberty become more firm and large and are especially designed by God to give the precise milk needed for a baby. The vulva is merely the term given to that portion surrounding the passage to the internal organs of reproduction.

The ovaries are two organs within the body which, after puberty, alternately produce one egg cell (ovum) each lunar (28-day) month. This tiny egg goes through a tube, is prepared for a meeting with the seed from the male (called conception), and goes finally into the womb (uterus). Meantime, the womb is preparing its lining for a possible pregnancy. If this does not take place, the egg is rejected with all this special preparatory material. This is called menstruation (menses, or monthlies), and it usually lasts several days. However, should conception take place, a baby begins to form, first in the tube, then passing to the uterus, where it is nourished. This tiny organism is first called an embryo, and later, when more mature, a fetus. It takes about nine months for a baby to develop in the womb, after which it is *delivered* through the vagina with considerable pain (labor). Up to the time of birth, a baby is attached to the mother at its navel or umbilicus.

The vagina is also the place which the male organ (penis) penetrates when depositing the seed. Just within the vulva and in the vagina are to be found the chief sources of female sexual pleasure in the marital act. Whenever the vulva regions and vagina begin to swell and exude a fluid, it is an indication of the beginning of sexual or venereal pleasure. This pleasure can increase to a climax or a series of climaxes followed by a very pleasurable relaxation of the muscles involved. This complete pleasure is called orgasm. Deliberately to bring about this pleasure by any means, outside of a lawful marriage act, is seriously sinful. If alone, this sin is called self-abuse or masturbation.

A girl should be instructed about menstruation in advance so that no emotional disturbance (fear, shock, etc.) will arise. She should be told of its purpose and normality, and also that it is a sign of her maturity. If in taking care of herself some venereal pleasure should arise, she must simply ignore it and refuse voluntarily to enjoy it (Moral Principle III). Before menstruation, or certainly at the first one, every mother should explain the correct hygienic procedure.[3]

Probably girls of 17 or over should know more about birth, for example, the kinds and frequency of labor pains, the process of birth, and so on. In the days when the home was also the birthplace, the older girls were expected to assist, and so learned most of these things. Now that hospitals are the usual place of birth, there is little opportunity to acquire this information. Certainly, a young married woman should be well instructed in these matters before her first pregnancy. Perhaps such instruction can be safely left until then.

How Much Should Each Sex Know of the Other?

The whole process of reproduction should be known by each sex at least by the time of maturity (18 as an outside limit), though of course it must be learned gradually. First, each child should know the names of its external organs (breasts, vulva; penis, scrotum). If there is any necessity or occasion to refer to sexual differences at an early age, the correct names may be used.

---

3. The companies that sell the various articles also have literature which will facilitate the mother's explanation (e. g., Personal Products Corporation, Milltown, New Jersey).

Then, gradually, each fact should slip into place. Though no absolute order can be laid down, since the needs of each child will vary, the following list of words indicates the usual *order* of learning the various facts of reproduction:

For the boy: Names of his external genitals (those of girls if occasion requires); origin of baby; purpose of breasts, womb, conception, egg (ovaries), seed (testes, nocturnal pollution), delivery, labor, vagina, intercourse (menstruation). The words in parenthesis indicate knowledge that may be dispensed with.

For the girl: Names of her external organs (those of boys if occasion requires); origin of baby, breasts and purpose, womb, conception, egg (ovaries), menstruation, seed (testes), delivery, labor, vagina, intercourse, penis. In giving these lists we do not necessarily mean that the words must be learned, but the facts behind them should be. The main thing is to put the ideas across!

These lists may be disputed or rearranged to meet any particular needs, but it seems to be the usual order of learning the gradual answers to the fundamental questions a child asks.

Minimum Facts

The essential "facts of life" can be phrased very simply in four statements:

1. There is a substance (life-giving fluid, material, etc.) in a man (seed) and a substance in a woman (egg) which, when united by a marriage embrace, may become a child. Menstruation and seminal emission are an indication of such power in each sex.

2. The marital embrace consists in a union of bodies for which the sex organs are designed. In this union the seed of the man is placed deep within the body of the woman. The pleasure connected with this act is a very intense one which God uses as a reward and inducement for the propagation of the human race.

3. The new baby develops for about nine months within the mother's body and is delivered through the vagina, the passage through which the seed originally traveled.

4. After birth, the baby is normally fed (nursed) at the mother's breasts.

Look through the preceding section with all its terminology. Is there any more information than is given in these four statements? We do not believe that any doctor, with all his detailed knowledge, can add any more "facts."

A CHILD'S BASIC QUESTIONS

There are really only five fundamental questions on sexual matters that children ask, and they are asked from only four basic points of view. If parents know simple answers to each of these questions and understand the child's approaches in proposing the questions, there is no reason why they cannot easily give the necessary information. The fundamental questions are these:

1. What are the bodily differences between boys and girls and why? (*Sexual differences*)

2. Where does the baby come from? (*Origin of life, Pregnancy*)

3. How does the baby get out? (*Childbirth*)

4. What is the new experience of puberty? *a*) *Menstruation; b*) *Seminal emission; c*) *Sexual arousal or excitement*)

5. How did the baby get there in the first place? (*Sexual intercourse*)

The virtue of chastity is concerned only with questions 4 *b*) and *c*), and 5. That is, it is concerned only with the ruling of sexual pleasure, experienced alone or with someone else. Therefore, these are the only questions that might cause anxiety. The subjects of questions 1, 2 and 3—pregnancy, childbirth, labor and nursing—after all do not directly pertain to the Sixth and Ninth Commandments; to venereal pleasure or sexual intercourse. They are not venereal activity, but its results. In explaining them to a child, therefore, try to prevent thoughts of venereal pleasure both in your mind and in his. Any temptation for the child that might arise from your answers to questions 1, 2 and 3 can arise only from a too vivid consideration of anatomy, which may be easily prevented by not emphasizing places in the body or raising graphic images of the body.

The four basic approaches to the above questions are the following:

1. *The ontological approach.* This is the point of view of the younger child, who is interested in origins, beginnings, causes, and not in the mechanics or pleasures of generation. He is awakening to a mysterious and beautiful world on which he wants information, and so arise the hundreds of "why" or "where" questions; for example, "Where did you get the twins, Mommy?" From this approach the child usually asks only questions 1 and 2. Rarely does he ask the others; and if he should, remember his reason for asking—just to discover the origins of things.

2. *The mechanical approach.* This is the approach of children just before adolescence (for example, from 9 to 12). Children of this age want to know something of how the body works and also the simple fact (and not the details) of sexual mating.[4] From this approach, the questions will be 1, 2, 3, 5; usually not 4. Even question 5 is asked for mechanical and not pleasurable reasons. Despite the fact that question 4 is not usually asked, at this age parents should take the oppor-

---

4. Cf. Strain, Frances Bruce, *New Patterns in Sex Teaching* (Appleton-Century, New York, 1934), pp. 139, 186.

tunity to prepare their youngsters for their first seminal emission or menstruation.

3. *The personal approach.* This is the approach of early adolescence (13 to 15). It is the point of view created by worry and anxiety over new feelings, new troubles, the awakening of self, and the first disturbing attraction to the other sex. *The* question which demands an answer is 4. If the earlier approaches have already been taken care of, this one will not be very hard. Since the child is trying to get some certainty, to get a grip on himself, he is frequently not too concerned about the function of the other sex. He is interested only in getting himself straightened out, in understanding and getting accustomed to these new sensations.

4. *The social approach.* This is the long, gradual approach from middle to late adolescence. Having made some adjustments in understanding himself, the adolescent begins to look toward social contacts with the other sex. As a result, he now wishes to obtain the sexual knowledge concerning relations with others. There are really no new questions, but only a re-ordering of information. The characteristic is curiosity about the functions of the other sex. (For example, the use of sanitary pads, why a girl gets "sick," the use of an athletic supporter, etc.)

Though each basic approach may demand a brief review of the previous instruction, it is during this last phase that review and consolidation of the facts, attitudes, moral and religious principles, are most needed. It seems to us that this is the only place in which a pamphlet might be helpful for the youngster to read.

THE QUESTIONS AND SOME ANSWERS

Some suggestions are in order, to enable you to answer these questions. You are reminded, however, that the suggestions are not final, nor necessarily in the progressive order in which the child will ask. You must vary the questions and the order to meet the needs of each child, according to his age and the approach that he uses.

Q. 1. What are the bodily differences between boys and girls, and why?

A. a) Allow the children below 6 to be present at the bath of the youngest. Casually mention that God makes little boys different from little girls, and that they grow up to be men and women. Take care also that they know that there are only *two* kinds of people, for occasionally children wonder whether there are not more than two kinds. Take care also that the younger children do not think their little brother or sister deformed because of these sexual differences.

b) Bathe young children (5 or less) together, commenting only if asked.

c) In connection with the later question concerning the marital act, explain that the male organ fits into the female organ of reproduction. (Cf. the answers to Q. 5.)

Q. 2. Where did the baby come from?

A. a) God sent us the baby.

b) From a little nest, bower, garden, jewel box, room, etc., beneath Mother's heart.

c) From the place beneath Mother's heart called the "womb." (Explanation of the Hail Mary.)

d) From the organ in Mother's abdomen called the "womb" or "uterus."

e) This information plus a little explanation regarding ovaries, etc., either in connection with the puberty instruction, or separately.

Q. 3. How does the baby get out?

A. a) God places an opening in Mother's body which

enlarges to let the baby out.

b) There is a channel, canal or hallway which opens to let the baby through.

c) The baby comes out of a kind of bodily door, or like a train through a tunnel.

d) This opening is in the lower part of the body trunk, in front.

e) It is the same passage (or hallway) through which the seed passes (or is deposited or placed). (In connection with puberty instruction.)

Q. 4. What is menstruation?

A. a) After a time a girl becomes mature, and develops into a young woman. This brings with it a new experience. You see, a girl has within her an egg cell, which can become a baby. Each month this egg and all the material that might be needed to nourish a baby within her, is cast off by the system. This matter also has some blood in it, and the process lasts several days. Don't be alarmed when this happens to you, for it is a sign that you are at last growing up to be a young woman. When this happens come to me, and I will explain further and tell you what to do.

b) The same, plus brief information concerning the contribution of the male element.

c) Add some general ideas of how the male contribution is made. (Cf. 1 c and answers to Q. 5.)

Q. 5. How did the baby get there?

A. a) God put him there.

b) The love of Mother and Daddy, blessed by God, put him there.

c) There is a substance in the bodies of mothers and fathers which together make the baby. This substance in fathers is called the seed and in mothers the egg.

d) An intimate (or deep) union of the parents' bodies is needed to form the body of a child by bringing the seed and the egg together. Remember that the parents are working with God, sharing His work of creation.

e) According to God's plan, the father and mother share in the production of a human body. That is why certain parts of a man's body are different from a woman's. (These different parts are called sexual parts.) They contain the seeds of life. It is by their union that the two seeds (or seed and egg) join together to grow into the body of a child.

f) The father's cells are placed deep within the body of the mother so they can move upward in search of an egg cell. (This is sexual union.)

g) A virgin (speak of Our Lady) is a woman who has not had the bodily relations with a man which lead to her becoming a mother (or, which lead to the birth of a child).

h) By a marital (or marriage) embrace, the seed is placed within the body of a wife by her husband.

i) The seed which joins the egg to form a baby is placed in an opening in the body of a woman.

j) Marital intercourse means the entrance of the private organ of a man into the private organ of a woman, and a flow of seed from the man's body into the woman's.

k) In marital intercourse, the penis of the male enters the vagina of the woman and deposits the semen (seed) there.

When?

Parents all ask: "When shall I give each piece of information?" After reading so many pages, you will know there is no definite answer. Each child has its own needs. He should get his answer when he needs it, no sooner, no later. However, a few norms may be laid down:

1. A child should always know truly where the baby comes from. Whenever that question is asked, it should be answered. The thought that a baby is in a nest

beneath the mother's heart will hardly create venereal pleasure. How baby gets out is another question. One may answer: "Doctor takes care of that." "There is an opening that enlarges to let baby out." "God provides an opening," etc. There seems to be no reason why they should know more; yet if they are further "enlightened" by playmates, always tell them the truth!

2. At entrance to the sixth grade for girls, and seventh for boys, the minimum facts (p. 156) should be given, minus the *details* of the marital embrace, for it it is enough if they know some kind of bodily union is involved. The instruction at this time should center on preparing them for their first menstruation period or seminal emission.

3. At puberty, the first seminal emission or menstruation, the same facts may be given with the emphasis on their own experiences rather than on those of the opposite sex. They have enough to do if they are to meet and conquer the first stirrings of the flesh.

4. About the age of 16, a more complete review may be in order, with some direction toward the opposite sex and possible future marriage. If a booklet will help, it is in order here, but first read it yourself to see whether it is of value for *this* child.

5. By the age of 18, both sexes may safely know all that is contained in the *complete* outline above (pp. 151-156). At this age they should know nearly all they are going to know for life, except the concrete, practical, physical adjustments they will need for their own marriages. If their physiology course contains the necessary facts, there is no need for parents to make certain they have the complete information.

How?

By this time you know that we do not believe anyone can tell you the "hows." No book or booklet seems satisfactory, simply because the instructors and children are different in every case. *There are no universal formulas,* but we can list a few helps:

1. In physiology, use the word "you" as seldom as possible. Make the instruction impersonal. If you talk of "men and women," "husband and wife," rather than "Mother and Dad," when explaining strictly sexual activity, the child will understand you and embarrassment will be avoided for all. A boy knows he is going to be a man, and a girl knows she is going to be a woman, but that seems ages off to both. Sex privileges should be made to seem equally in the distant future, for sexual acts are for the married alone. Youth will make the personal application as needed.

2. It is always easier to handle the problem of sex information if the child asks the questions as they come to him. But a child may not ask questions. What then? To begin with, you must, if possible, find out *why* the child does not question you. This can happen for a number of reasons.

First, the child may not have confidence in you. In that case, you can do little but attempt to create confidence, or direct the child to someone he does trust.

Secondly, a child may not be interested. Then leave him alone! Perhaps you might give him a few leading sentences from time to time, but don't force information on him.

Lastly, a child may be afraid to ask, either because he fears you will but confirm the disgusting stories he has already heard, or because he vaguely realizes the obligations connected with sex and is afraid to face them.

On discovering the first reason, give him the true, beautiful and religious explanation, leading into it with some such phrases as: "I suppose you have heard the boys discussing these things. I'm sorry you heard it that way. It is so false a picture," etc. If you discover the second reason, try over a period of months to bring the child to face his responsibilities at least sufficiently to help him meet the crisis of each stage, for example, puberty, adolescence, etc.; even, should it be necessary, "sit him down and give it to him straight."

In all cases of this kind, if you are forced to ask such leading questions as: "Do you know where babies come from?", etc., do not take, "Yes," for an answer. Youngsters in these circumstances will almost always answer "Yes." In many cases they could truly answer "No," for they do not really know enough to understand the question! Your child may know something, but is it correct knowledge? In such a case, you can return: "Well, then, you know that babies come from their mothers' bodies," etc., etc.

3. The coming of a new baby is an opportunity. Some mothers allow their young children to feel the stirrings of life in their abdomen. Can you think of a good reason for forbidding this?

4. Give your older girls the care of the babies—the bathing and changing. They learn the double lesson of anatomical differences and child care.

5. Take examples from the world around as they present themselves in the life of a child. Nan, in *Never No More,* already quoted, used the damming of a stream to explain the preparatory function in the uterus and the resulting menstruation (p. 62). She used sowing of seed in farming to explain "the father's part" (p. 64). Incidentally, the instruction described in this novel, though not entirely complete, is adequate despite the fact that it does not use a single physical term other than "seed."

6. At the end of every instruction, especially if it is lengthy, give the child a thought or an occupation which will take his mind away from the subject. (But do not be too obvious about it!) If, for any reason, a sex instruction is needed near bedtime, make sure there is

some other thought to dream about.

7. If a child seems anxious about an experience of pleasure in the sexual organs, tell him: "That pleasure is to be used only in marriage. There it is good and holy." He will begin to see the reason for it, where it is right and where wrong. Never let a boy or girl think that sex pleasure is *always* and *everywhere* sinful.

8. The proper names for their external sex organs can be easily learned at bath time. Merely say: "Wash your vulva carefully," etc. No direct reference should be made such as, "This is the penis and is used. . . ."

9. As mentioned above, very young children of both sexes may be bathed together. Without realizing it, they will familiarize themselves with sex differences. Of course they will forget this, but some vague impressions will remain which will make later instruction easier. It may seem difficult to discontinue this mixed bathing, but it should be done and can in fact be done easily. As the older child goes to school at the age of 6, simply make it a point to bathe the younger ones alone during school time. Some object to this practice of mixed bathing, on the grounds that children should not do now what they will later be forbidden to do. There is some reason behind this objection, and since our recommendation is not absolute, you may judge for yourself. However, it would seem to us to be more helpful, and the objection is not completely valid because a young child is not so easily tempted, and modesty is not an absolute but a relative affair. Indeed, there are times when adults may appear disrobed before others, even of the other sex; for example, before a doctor.

10. A question arises about teaching sex from flowers, birds, bees, and animals. We insist that questions which the child may ask about them should be answered. Yet it seems clear to us that these facts of plant and animal reproduction *should not be used to teach about human reproduction*. Even married people

occasionally have wrong notions from their observation of animals. However, *as a broader setting,* knowledge of animal reproduction may be of help in understanding human reproduction. Some suggest that, when a chicken is being cleaned, eggs within the body be shown to children as an example. They also recommend having pets (love birds, dogs, rabbits, etc.) which children can observe. We are not at all opposed to their being interested in pets and asking questions about them; yet the answers should only indicate reference to the pets, not to human reproduction. Some children know a great deal about animals and do not transfer it at all. "Facts of human life" will still be needed. Besides all this, pets are not human, do not "love" in the human sense, and are not governed by moral and religious principles.

It has also been recommended that children be given an occasion to observe animals in sexual acts and in labor. We do not think this advisable. Should children notice these things without their attention being directed to them, be prudent, because a great deal of delicacy is required. Do not snatch them away hurriedly or guiltily lest they become all the more curious. Perhaps it might be better to ignore the whole situation if it cannot be avoided. This is a problem worthy of discussion.

11. Always be casual, unashamed, frank, sincere and reverent in giving sex instruction. Even an unintentional mistake in instruction (too soon, too detailed) will do little harm if confidence is not shattered.

12. *Never give a fact without a correct attitude,* religious, moral or emotional. Every sex instruction should be correlated with some part of God's plan, the supernatural purposes of sex, etc. For instance, use the Hail Mary ("womb"); the Angelus ("and she conceived"); the Immaculate Conception; the nine months' time from Annunciation, March 25, to Christmas; and from December 8 (Immaculate Conception) to September 8 (Nativ-

ity of Our Lady); the Virginity of Mary; the Annunciation story, "I do not know man."[5]

13. Rarely take a child aside for sex instruction. Introduce the facts when needed—while washing dishes, on a hike, working together, etc. Only a really pressing problem which needs serious attention, such as sin or great difficulty in temptation, will demand a special session. In such a case, an adolescent will appreciate your more serious and formal approach, because you are complimenting him by treating him as an adult.

14. Our insistence on true answers does not mean that information may not be refused on occasion. Some adolescents will ask questions until they have all the information which you as married people possess. If questions go beyond the need of the individual, withhold the answers and explain why; that is, the danger to purity outweighs the advantage of the knowledge. Every child should know (and act according to the knowledge) that not all things about any subject can be investigated or are worth investigating at one time. Let adolescents learn due prudence in questioning. Though you need not scold them when they fail in this respect, indicate the present danger of some facts which can be better understood later. The norm for proper questions is the Third Moral Principle, whereas the norm for prudent answers is the Fourth.

15. Many people fear the danger of shocking a child by sexual information. We have indicated the nature of shock above (Chapter IV, p. 39), and have shown how shock can be avoided by a gradual approach and a reverent attitude. Should it occur, do not worry about it. A "pardon me" will usually suffice because each one knows that no family member wishes to wound or shock another. Wait until the shock has abated, then apologize and return to the subject as cautiously as necessary.

---

5. Cf. Juergens, Sylvester P., S. M., *Fundamental Talks on Purity,* Bruce, Milwaukee, 1941.

16. In general, sexual instruction of boys should be quite different from that given to girls, which fact demands an understanding of their emotional natures. First, girls like a lovingly romantic, beautiful approach, while boys are apt to want to "get down to brass tacks." Secondly, boys will have more difficulty with personal purity than will girls. Consequently, with a boy, approach the problem as quickly and easily as possible. Don't build up lengthily before you slip the idea across, and ordinarily avoid prefacing your remarks by, "Now, I'm going to tell you about sex." If you keep telling him you are going to tell him, you may stir up his passions. He knows something of what you are going to say and the suspense will be too great. On the other hand, girls need a smoother, longer approach to avoid shock. Consequently, examples of mother love and other things pertaining to the idealistic side of sex, should be injected. Also, for the girls, the approach may well be less specific on physical pleasure. In general, then (depending always on the individual), less approach is needed for the boy, but more specific information; for the girl, more approach and less specific information.

Whatever you think of this hint, you will at least agree that an identical instruction should not be given to both sexes. Compare, for example, the two completely different models in Bruckner's *How To Give Sex Instruction*.[6] Contrast with them the nearly identical ones for boys and girls in Juergens' *Fundamental Talks on Purity*, already cited.

17. Try always to see things with the child's mind. Put yourself in his place, at his age, with his temperament. Then you will understand his questions and give satisfactory answers. If you don't know what his questions mean to him, find out indirectly *first.* Counter his questions with another: "What makes you ask that?" "What do you mean?" Otherwise, you will err as a mother once did who gave her child a whole detailed

---

6. The Queen's Work, St. Louis, 1937.

heart-to-heart talk when he asked, "Where did I come from?" She did not try to find out what the question meant. After the full explanation of the process of generation, the child sighed in bewilderment: "All that! And Jimmy only came from Brooklyn!"

18. Should a youngster burst in on you with some crude and unprintable four-letter word, be careful! Your first impulse will be to wash his mouth out with soap, and explain nothing—a sad mistake. First, find out if he knows what the word means. If he does, tell him the acceptable term or terms and explain that the one he used has an obscene, vulgar and disgusting tone and is never used by chaste people. If the youngster does not know the meaning of this word, merely explain its vulgarity in a general way and forbid it. Should this expedient merely create itching curiosity, explain all as in the first case.

CASES FOR DISCUSSION

1. Michael, a boy of 12, while at the zoo, noticed two small animals in coitus. He went over to his dad and asked, "What are they doing?" His dad said, "Oh, just fooling around!"

What would you have answered with all that crowd surrounding you? How would this be: "They do that when they want puppies (kittens, young, little ones, etc.). I'll tell you about it some time." Later the father could explain that a fluid passes from the male to female and this produces the little ones.

If a 6-year-old asked the above question, answer: "Shows they are in love, it's a hug of affection"; or, "That's the way they show affection."

2. Pat, aged 5, said: "Mommy went to the hospital fat and came back thin. Why?" Suggested answer: "Well, she brought fat little Joe back with her. You see, babies grow inside of mothers just as if they were in a nest. They are kept warm and safe until they're big enough

to come out and have you play with them."

3. Jean, aged 4: "Why didn't Mommy go to the hospital to have a baby this Christmas; she did last year?"

Suggestion: "It wouldn't be much fun if everyone had a birthday at the same time, would it?" (Notice that this question is not at all concerned with sex, and the answer recognizes that not every question along these lines demands a "facts of life" reply.)

4. George, aged 7: "Mom, how can you tell Aunt Belle is going to the hospital in two months? She's kind of fat, but she looks all right to me."

Suggestion: Tell George that Aunt Belle is going to have a baby. Explain that the baby in its nest takes nine months to grow, so the mother knows about when it is ready to be born; she can feel its weight and even its stirring. Recall St. John Baptist's "leap of joy" in Elizabeth's womb when Mary came with Jesus in her womb.

5. Joan, aged 4: "Mommy, what's being born?"

Suggestion: "It's being let out of the mother's nest" (when child already knows about womb).

6. Ellen, aged 6-1/2, in a rush: "Mother, did I come out of your stomach?"

Suggestion: "Well, Ellen, all little girls come out of their mothers' stomachs." (Why not merely "Yes"? Because that leaves things on a too personal basis. "All little girls" is better.)

Ellen: "Well, how do they get out?"

Suggestion: "Mothers go to hospitals to have babies. Doctors know a lot more than we do. They take care of that." Or, "God places an opening in mothers' bodies which enlarges to let the baby out."

7. Marie, aged 14, had just experienced her first menstruation. She was terrified, since she had not been prepared for it. She went to her mother, who calmed her and explained matters. After telling her methods

of caring for herself, she added: "And now be doubly careful with men. You are old enough to have a baby now."

Marie knew having a baby out of marriage was a sin, so for months she was afraid to come within six feet of a man! What was wrong with this instruction? Try phrasing one yourself. Should not some idea of a bodily *union* have been indicated, however vaguely?

8. Joe, aged 15, was called aside by his uncomfortable father for a heart-to-heart talk. "Well, Joe, I suppose you know all about where babies come from?" (*Gulp.*) "Ye-es," answered Joe. "Well, then, there's no need to talk. Just be careful and pure. You're growing up to be a man now." Did Joe's "yes" indicate knowledge? How would you go about it?

9. Jack, aged 13, awoke one night to find himself experiencing his first seminal emission. He was greatly frightened by this experience. How would you reassure him and explain? Shouldn't he have been sufficiently prepared at least to recognize this reaction when it came?

10. Mae, a mother, was obviously pregnant. Her 5-1/2-year-old son, Don, starting asking questions.

Don: "Mother, why is your stomach so big?"

Mae: "We are going to have a baby. It is growing beneath my heart. It was a tiny seed and is now getting bigger." Don: "How did the seed get there?"

Mae: "It was planted there."

Don: "Who planted it there?"

Mae: "Daddy did."

Don: "How, etc.?"

Should this mother have gone so far with a child of this age? Would it not have been better to stop at the word "heart" in her first answer? Would it not have been better to answer, "God put it there," and let the matter drop? This mother gave no caution, so Don blurted out the news to his friends. Should it have been a family secret? Can children keep secrets?

11. Don't be surprised if you do not get complete agreement in your discussions. These cases demand prudent decisions, and prudent decisions cannot be absolutely and universally certain. A majority decision should give a good norm. You have learned much if you have learned *ease* in discussion, and the choice of good words. At times your particular personality or your knowledge of your own child in certain circumstances will make your decision different from that of others. But if you are *always* in disagreement with the majority, be cautious; there may be something that should be corrected in your point of view.

QUESTIONS AND DISCUSSION AIDS

1. Does technical terminology stifle sexual temptation? Does it satisfy curiosity? Does virtue always flow from knowledge?

2. What conclusions have you drawn concerning teaching your children the correct names from the beginning? Is a great deal of physiological knowledge needed by married people? Should sexual physiology be omitted from high school physiology courses? Give reasons.

3. Without looking at our outline, try to phrase a reasonably complete instruction on the "facts of life." Discuss it with the others in your group. Then compare it with our outline.

4. What are the five basic questions of a child? The four basic approaches? Is this division really helpful? Try to phrase answers in your own words.

5. What should you do if the child does not ask questions?

6. Why is it important to indicate to a child that there is a place where sexual pleasure is right and holy?

7. Why is it important to use totally different instructions for boys and girls?

8. Bring up all the problems you have already faced with your children and try to analyze them in the light of what you have learned. If there are any problems which do not seem to be answered in this chapter, please send them to the author in care of the Confraternity of Christian Doctrine.

9. After you have discussed the suggestions in this chapter, compare your solutions with the following instruction which was composed by a group of Cana Couples using the same material as is contained in this book.

SUGGESTIONS FOR INSTRUCTING CHILDREN
ON MOTHERHOOD AND FATHERHOOD

(TO BE GIVEN TO THE CHILD BIT BY BIT FROM EARLIEST
YEARS TILL ABOUT 11)

How does a baby come into the world? Let's see. . . .

God made the world by Himself— God made some things *all by Himself*— as when He made the world, with the sun and moon and stars, the flowers and the trees and the animals. So also, when God made the first two people, Adam and Eve, He made them all by Himself, and nobody helped Him.

but He lets man help Him make children But God did something wonderful for those first two people: *He let them help Him* make their children. And ever since that time, God has let men and women help Him to bring children into the world. God was very good to do this, for He didn't need the help of people; He could have made all children the way He made Adam and Eve, without anybody's help. But because God loves people and wants to make them happy and proud to be His partner, He lets them help Him in the wonderful work of making a child. Just think, if God had let people help Him make the world, with the sky and the sun and the trees, how proud and happy they would feel to be God's partners! But God does even more than this. . . . He lets people help Him make babies, who will live forever in Heaven with God, long after the world has ended.

Three required: father— mother— God

So you see, it takes *three* to make a baby: the father, the mother, and God. If any one of them is missing, there is no baby . . . all three have to join in. What do the father and mother do? They make the baby's body. And what does God do? He makes the baby's soul, that gives it its life.

Origin of cells

How do the father and mother make the baby's body? Let me tell you. First of all, I must tell you that the baby's body is made from two tiny living things like seeds, called cells. One of these little cells is in the body of the father, and the other little cell is in the body of the mother.

Womb

Now, inside the mother's body there is a little room, called the womb (*a pat will indicate the place*). This little room in the mother is going to be the baby's home for about the first nine months of its life. (Mary had a little room like this in her body, too, and that's where Jesus lived for the first nine months of His life. Remember the words in the Hail Mary, "Blessed is the fruit of thy womb"? These words tell about this little room in Mary's body.)

Cell-union   The mother's cell is in this room; the
(conception) father's cell comes into this room and
meets the mother's cell, and then these
two little cells join together and become
one cell. This is called conception. When
the two cells join together, God puts a
soul there with life . . . and that is the
beginning of a baby.

Organs   But how does the cell of the father get
into that little room in the mother, where
her cell is? Well, there is a little opening
in the mother's body, right below her stomach; this opening is like a little hallway
or passage going to that room in her body.
The Now the father has a part of his body
father's like a little tube; when this tube enters
part the hallway of the mother, the father's
cell passes through this tube into the
mother's hallway, and keeps on going
until it comes into the little room of the
mother, where her cell is waiting. As I
told you, these two little cells then join
together and become one, and God gives
it a soul with life . . . and a tiny baby
has started to live.[7]

Jesus born   (Jesus, too, lived in such a little room
of the in the body of the Blessed Virgin Mary
Virgin before He was born. But only Mary helped
Mother God make Jesus' body . . . no human father helped God to do this—just Mary
and God. That's why we call Mary "the
Virgin Mother.")

---

7. To prevent confusion and vulgar ideas, it may be helpful to explain that the two
functions of voiding and of generation, while using the same external bodily out-
lets, are entirely distinct functions, with entirely different internal channels which
cannot function at the same time.

Pregnancy

So you see, the baby is very tiny when it first begins to live in its mother, in that little room which is its first home. It lives there for about nine months, and during that time it grows and becomes bigger, and its mother becomes rounder, until finally the baby is ready to be born. During these nine months the mother often thinks about her baby and loves it, hoping for the day when it will be born and she can hold it in her arms. The daddy, too, looks forward to the baby's coming, and watches over the mother during this time, because he loves the baby which he helped to make. Also God watches over the mother and baby, for He, too, loves the baby to which He gave life.

Birth

How does the baby come out of the mother and be born? It is very simple. The baby, who has been in the little room of the mother, now comes through that same hallway, which can stretch enough to let the baby through—and the baby is very little anyhow! Usually the mother goes to a hospital, where a doctor helps the baby to be born, and takes care of the mother.

Parent's joy

When the baby is born, it is put into its mother's arms right away. Both she and the daddy look down with great joy and happiness at the little child that God has given them. The baby belongs to both of them, and it also belongs to God . . . really, God gave them this baby to take care of for Him, so that some day it could come to Him in Heaven. The daddy and mother gladly take care of it for God, because they love the baby and because they also love God.

Nursing

At first, when the baby is very small, it can't eat all the things you eat. It is so little and weak that it needs special food. This special food is the milk in the mother's breasts, which the baby gets when the mother nurses it. Wasn't God good to think of everything for the baby?

Baptism

But God doesn't only want to give life to the baby's *body* so that it can live on earth; He also wants to give a very special life to its *soul,* so that the baby can live in Heaven after it dies. So, a short time after the baby is born, it is taken to church and is baptized by a priest. Through this Baptism God gives His life to the baby's soul, so that it can live with Him in Heaven. This special life of the soul is called God's grace. From the day it's baptized, the baby is a child of God and belongs to God's Church.

Only in marriage

God wants people to help Him make children; but only when they are married, because a child needs a home where the father and mother will take care of it. If people just had children without getting married and making a home, the children would have no home and nobody to look after them, and give them the love they need. Wouldn't it be horrible if little boys and girls didn't have mothers and fathers to love them as they grow up? So, you see, for people to have children without being married would be very wrong and a big sin.

A work of love

Don't you think that it's very wonderful how a baby comes into the world? It is all done through love. A man and a woman love each other very much, and want to be together all their lives. So they get married. But they also want others to have their love and happiness. So they have babies. The daddy and mother know that some day their babies will go to Heaven and be happy forever with God . . . and that's really the main reason why they want babies. If your daddy and mother hadn't had you, you wouldn't be here now, and you wouldn't be able to get to Heaven. Do you see how much they loved you?

Some day you

Some day God may let you help Him, and you will be the daddy (mother) of lovely babies. So you see that we all come from God at the beginning of our lives, and we all go back to God at the end of our lives, to be happy forever. God surely does love us!

Chapter XII

Dangers to Purity

Though we might prefer to have our children ignorant as long as possible of all evil, and especially of the evils of impurity, ignorance can become, after a certain age, a trap for the unwary. In our modern pagan surroundings, with the allurements to sexual pleasure painted on all sides, due warning must *anticipate* the chief dangers at each step of the child's development. It would certainly be criminal to allow a child or an adolescent to fall into dangers he is not prepared for.

Now, though warnings should be sufficiently accurate to enable a child to recognize a danger when it comes, they should not be so detailed as to *create* the very peril we wish to avoid. After the first more general admonitions, a road must be left open for further questions and further instructions when more particular dangers are met.

The obligation of pointing out the dangers to purity rests chiefly on the shoulders of parents, for they are responsible for the spiritual as well as the bodily welfare of their children. However, both priests and teachers have the obligation to extend and complete these warnings because they too have serious responsibility for the moral welfare of their charges. Pope Pius XII, in *Guiding Christ's Little Ones,* points out the value of these precautions when he tells parents (p. 11):

> Your words, if they are wise and discreet, will prove a safeguard and a warning in the midst of the temptations

179

and corruption which surround them "because, foreseen, an arrow comes more slowly."

WHAT DANGERS?

A solid moral theologian gives us a good outline for this type of instruction.[1] Here is a rough translation of what he says:

Boys and girls should be cautiously instructed, whenever occasion arises, on the morality of some acts and the immorality of others; for example, that bodily needs may be met without sin, despite the presence of involuntary pleasure, but that unnecessary handling of the genitals is dangerous and more or less sinful. Adolescents who go to high school, or into military service, factories, offices, domestic service, nursing, etc., should be instructed about the chief perils to which their virtue may be exposed. Particularly should they be told of the malice of masturbation, fornication and adultery. It may not be necessary that they know these words, but they must know the facts behind them; that is, that venereal pleasure is sinful outside of marriage, and that the marital act is a crime except between two persons married to each other.

It is our conviction that parents are far more capable of judging particular dangers than anyone else. They live in the world, work in the factories and offices, hear the conversations, and see the actions. It is their duty to note the evils and to give proper warnings to their children. On our part, we shall list the chief headings under which these dangers fall.

---

1. Aertnys-Damen, *op. cit.*, I, # 496, q. 2.

VENEREAL DISEASES

Venereal diseases are frequently the results of impurity, and therefore we include them for brief notice in this chapter. The danger of venereal disease is very real but cannot be depended upon as a great deterrent to sexual sin. Few young people would remain chaste were fear their only motive, for the allurements of sexual experimentation would easily outweigh the fear. However, since these diseases are so widespread, it is well to give adequate instruction regarding them.

In the beginning, there is no need to point out the scourge of venereal diseases directly. Merely teach the child to act with proper care in public bathrooms and to avoid the common drinking cup or towel. Luckily, our modern methods of hygiene have to a large degree eliminated these means of spreading such diseases, but the precautions must be taught nonetheless. They will slip easily into the child's training in general hygiene.[2] Later, the nature of syphilis and gonorrhea may be calmly explained.

These are diseases chiefly of the sexual organs, and are extremely painful and infectious. Either may cause sterility; or the persons infected may produce diseased and defective children. Syphilis may even progress so far as to cause insanity and death. Only recently have there been advances dealing with these scourges. At the present time, if they are detected early enough, they may be cured, or at least rendered dormant and non-infectious. Finally, adolescents in their late teens should be told that these diseases are usually contracted by illicit sexual intercourse. It is *possible,* of course, that they be contracted in marriage, or by disregarding the laws of hygiene already described. However, it must be stressed that there is practically no danger to those persons who refrain from sexual rela-

---

2. Hygiene is simply the science and practice of health preservation. When one avoids disease by the practice of cleanliness, antisepsis, etc., he is practicing the art of personal hygiene.

tions except with a healthy spouse, and who are reasonably trained in the rules of common-sense hygiene.

Because venereal diseases may be contracted innocently in marriage, it is wise to advise a physical examination of both parties before marriage. There are many other advantages to the practice. A willingness to have this physical examination is not an admission of impurity, for such procedures ought to be considered routine, a pledge of love and regard for a future partner.[3]

PERSONAL IMMODESTY

In Oneself

Teach children a routine in dressing and undressing which will expose them as little and as briefly as is reasonably possible. Teach them also to avoid too much curiosity about their own sex. Though it will rarely be sinful to see the sexual organs of one's own sex, there is some danger. Let them understand that once a reasonable amount of knowledge is obtained, further curiosity is dangerous, and that this type of curiosity will never be satisfied.

Another danger is the unnecessary handling of the genitals, which may induce masturbation. However, a word of caution. Some may think that "necessary" means absolute necessity; that is, what is required to remain alive! No, whatever is needful for cleanliness, health, dressing, comfort, etc., is perfectly legitimate.

Modesty of eyes as well as of touch is a "must" for Catholics today. In this connection it is necessary to warn adolescents about the evil effects of obscene, sexy and pornographic books, magazines, photographs, movies, plays and burlesque shows. Show them also the sinfulness in "necking" and "petting," etc., which are so prominently featured in modern literature. Tell them frankly what is sinful in such things.

---

3. Further information on this whole subject will be found in *The Venereal Diseases,* by Thurman B. Rice, American Medical Association, Chicago, 1939.

With Others

One has obligations to others, whether of the same or opposite sex. Teach children what these obligations are. Above all, explain to adolescent girls what effect immodest dress and behavior has upon men. Besides being a danger to others, lack of modesty in this respect may cause misery to oneself—not all sex crimes are entirely the fault of the aggressor! Again, in their desire to be attractive, girls must not imitate sinful women. If they dress and act as such, they have only themselves to blame if they are accepted as such.

With Playmates

Tell children they are never to allow intimacies of touch by their playmates. Keep a wary eye on children for some types of games, for example, "playing doctor." Also be cautious about trips to the bathroom in common. And finally, after babyhood, the two sexes obviously should not be allowed to sleep in the same room, or at least not in the same bed.

PERVERSION BY ELDERS

It should be an inviolable rule that your children should never be alone, or go alone, with a stranger, whether man or woman. The dangers of sexual perversion and worse are rampant. J. Edgar Hoover says that this crime "is taking its toll at the rate of a criminal assault every forty-three minutes day and night in the United States."[4] This rule should hold from babyhood through adolescence for both boys and girls. Any violation of obedience in the matter should draw instant and severe punishment. If necessary, tell the older children why. Many adolescents will not heed such warnings without hearing the reasons.

---

4. See the *American Magazine* for July, 1947, p. 32: "How Safe Is Your Daughter?" Quoted with permission of the publisher.

To quote again from the Hoover article: "Parents should iterate and reiterate that their children, boys or girls, should not accept money or favors from strange men or women, and, above all, should never get in a car with a stranger or visit a stranger's home" (p. 104). Be consistent in this matter. If your child should go along with someone who is a stranger to him and who finally turns out to be an old friend, don't just smile! Despite the happy outcome, the child has violated your rule. And if, on the other hand, a child refuses a ride with strangers who happen to be long-lost cousins, he should be commended, not laughed at!

In connection with the danger of perversion, be wide awake about the places your children frequent. Local movie houses, gymnasiums, playgrounds, bath houses, etc., are all possible hunting grounds for perverts. Occasionally, even though rarely, a gym instructor or instructress is at fault. Do not have ugly suspicions without reason—but do not be too skeptical if your child, perhaps without knowing how, tries to tell you that something is wrong!

LATE HOURS

For the same reasons—that is—the possible dangers to personal purity, dangers which may include perversion—do not allow late hours to adolescents unless the circumstances are extraordinary. In general, the only place for an adolescent after ten is bed! Next, make sure that dances and get-togethers are under sound auspices, and try to have the young people come and go in groups. Then, recall that automobiles also bring dangers. Two or three couples (boys in front seat, girls in back) are safer than single couples.

Lastly, it may be necessary to indicate the brutal danger of rape. We dislike to mention the fact, but it has been privately estimated (from figures limited to *reported* crimes, not those which have not come to light) that one in each 1,850 city women under 30 in the

United States is liable to rape within a year! Does this frighten you? We hope it will, at least to the extent of inducing you to take sensible precautions for your children's welfare.

SCHOOLS

Dangers unfortunately continue to exist in schools, particularly high schools. Gyms, bathrooms and shower rooms furnish some perils. Others are found in the jokes being told, and the crude distortions of the "facts of life" going about. Still others are found in the new interest in so-called "humor," and "spice" magazines. Finally, both professional and non-professional salesmen for these and other obscene devices are sometimes found haunting the school grounds. Due warnings concerning these dangers are in order.

Boarding schools also offer occasions for sin. Where (as is mainly the case) such a school is only for boys, or only for girls, the danger usually comes from a schoolmate of the same sex. (Occasionally even a teacher or employee may be at fault.) Such danger may possibly be greater in schools for girls, but it exists almost equally in schools for boys. Since girls are by nature given to emotional love, without realizing what it may lead to, they are more easily betrayed. At any rate, it seems necessary to warn both sexes against allowing any intimate touch.

WORK

You will easily recognize the dangers in places of employment: the washrooms; the amorous employer; the paternal dispenser of rides home, not-too-good books, etc. You will probably think of more of these than we can name!

Secondly, it is also well to warn the young worker against the invitation to a "good time." Let young men or women find out what the "good time" is to consist of before accepting such an invitation. If it is to be a mixed party of girls and boys, let them find out what is to be done when the party meets. This need for wariness about a "good time" holds especially for those in military service. Chaplains have mentioned their conviction that a number of young men have been betrayed into sins because of their ignorance of what a "good time" could mean, and their "shame of being ashamed" when they found out.

How?

In all of the above, it is difficult to say what is to be told and what merely hinted. The decision will always be difficult in any given case. Tell children enough so that they will recognize the temptation, however vaguely, for what it is. If they know the warning signals, they need not know the specific danger. Yet, if they refuse to heed the warning signals, they must be told of the danger. It cannot be too strongly stated that this is a serious parental duty. Should an adolescent fall into sin because he lacks sufficient knowledge of the pitfalls, his parents are responsible.

The Positive Approach

There can be no doubt that for centuries there have been devilish snares laid to destroy the innocence of youth. St. Peter remarked it when he said: "Be sober, be watchful! For your adversary the devil, as a roaring lion, goes about seeking someone to devour" (*1 Ptr.* 5:8). Pope Pius XII brings the observation up to date when he tells parents: "You have to prepare your sons and daughters so that they may pass with unfaltering step like those who pick their way among serpents."[5] Therefore, parents must point out these perils, and must frequently phrase their warnings in "don'ts." On

---

5. *Guiding Christ's Little Ones*, p. 9.

the other hand, however, an exclusively negative set of rules can be harmful. If we stress the "don'ts" too much, we are liable to create an impression that purity is a gray, dull, crippling virtue which kills all the pleasure of life. Such an idea would certainly be false, for purity, though delicate, is a precious and joyful jewel which brings with it a content, peace and happiness nothing can equal; whereas impurity brings only gnawing discontent, disgust and dissatisfaction, despite the sensual pleasures enjoyed.

Try, therefore, to give a positive tone to all your instructions. Show the youngster the real value of purity first, and then your "don'ts" will fall on receptive ears. Once a boy recognizes the honor of holding a place on his school team, he will train. Once a boy begins to esteem purity and wishes to remain chaste, he will avoid the pitfalls. Teach adolescents how to regard this treasure of bodily and mental purity. Show them what it will mean to bring a pure body and mind into marriage. Indicate the peace and strength they will find in a chaste life. Tell them about the triumph Christ promised when He said: ". . . the kingdom of heaven has been enduring violent assault, and the violent have been seizing it by force" (*Matt.* 11:12).

Another error must be avoided in giving necessary warnings. Try not to cause *unwholesome* fear whether of the traps or of sex itself. At first sight the perils seem overwhelming, and a boy or girl might prefer to be free of chastity's burdensome treasure. It is true that no one can remain chaste except with God's help. Yet that help can be had for the asking. Again, the value of the generative powers is so great that it easily outweighs the burden of self-control. Hence, teach your children this holy wisdom:

> And as I knew that I could not otherwise be continent, except God gave it, and this also was a point of wisdom, to know whose gift it was: I went to the Lord and besought Him, and said with

my whole heart: . . . Give me wisdom (*Wis.* 8:21; 9:4).

Show them also St. Peter's confidence in divine providence, when he added this encouragement to the dreadful warning mentioned above: "Resist him [the devil], steadfast in the faith. . . . The God of all grace . . . will Himself, after we have suffered a little while, perfect, strengthen and establish us" (*1 Ptr.* 5:9-11).

Positive attitudes toward the dangers to purity can best be summed up in the following motto:

> *Caution,* not fear!
> *Confidence* in God, not despair!
> *Love for purity,* not distaste.

CASES FOR DISCUSSION

1. George, a boy of 16, worked after school in the mailing department of a large brokerage firm. As he went in a cab to the post office one day, the cab driver (about 40) asked George and another boy to go out with him and another man for a "good time" when their day's work was through. George refused on the ground that his mother would worry if he was not home by seven.

Suppose this were George's only reason, would that have outweighed the lure of an evening at an amusement park? Should George have suspected other plans? How would you warn your son in going to work on a similar job?

2. Joe, a boy of 14, accepted a ride home from a strange man. His mother told him not to do it again, saying, "Some men are worse than bad women, Joe." Did she say too much? Would you have courage to say the same?

3. Louise, a girl of 17, by an unforeseen set of circumstances was forced to come home alone on a street-

car at midnight. During the ride an older man kept eyeing her. As she got off at her transfer stop, he did too. Louise ran to the transfer place a block away. She felt safe only when she saw a group of people waiting for the second car.

Was she wise to run? Even granting that the man had no evil intentions, did Louise do well to play safe?

4. Mary, aged 16, was at a dance under the auspices of her C.Y.O. group. There she met a clean-cut boy, older than she, who eventually offered her a ride home in his father's car. She refused upon some pretext, and left later with a group of girls. The same boy drove up with another boy and offered the group a ride home. He opened the back door in invitation. Despite her reluctance, and with some protest, Mary got in with the other girls, and all got out together later. Did Mary do right in her first refusal? In her final acceptance? Did the boy's honest voice, his offer to the *group,* his offer of the back seat to them, the fact that he went to a Catholic high school, make any difference? Would Mary have been wise to continue the ride after the other girls got out? How would you have acted in her place? How would you advise your daughter?

5. Delia, aged 14, was in her first year of high school. She knew she was a rather pretty girl. The gym teacher tried frequently to have one girl or another stay behind after class, and seemed to prefer Delia. She later confessed that she did a lot of dodging to avoid this. An effort to tell her mother that something seemed wrong, she didn't know what, brought no response. The other girls frequently talked of this among themselves, but did not know what to do about it. Eventually one mother was awakened to activity, and the gym teacher passed on to other fields.

Would you have been as slow as Delia's mother? What would you have done? What and how much would you have told Delia?

6. John and Jim, aged 8 and 9, forced a girl of 7 to play "doctors' games" with them which involved nearly complete disrobing. Suppose John and Jim were your sons, what would you say? Do? What would be your proportion between reasons and punishment, if any?

7. Jean, aged 8, had taken a trolley ride to visit a friend. While she was waiting for the return trip, a car drew up and a man, who insisted he was her Uncle Jim, asked her to let him take her home. She knew she had an Uncle Jim, and this man seemed to know where she lived. She accepted the offer. It turned out that he was her uncle. Yet her mother spanked her soundly for disobedience to her mother's previous instructions, and gave her uncle quite a talking to.

Did Jean's mother act correctly? Would you have been so severe? Would a milder punishment have been justified because of the happy outcome? Suppose it had not been her Uncle Jim? How should Jean have answered her uncle?

8. Jack, 18, is going into the Army for his military training. Of what would your last man-to-man talk consist? Would the words "prostitute," "pin-up," "house of ill fame," "obscene pictures," or their equivalents, come up? If you were in either of the last two wars, would your own experiences help? Would it have made it any easier if your dad had given you such warnings?

9. Lulu, aged 17, likes to be attractive, and goes in for style and cosmetics. Her intentions are not in the least evil, but she follows the latest fashions in every department. She notices that the boys stare from time to time, and finally she is "propositioned." Lulu responds with an indignant refusal. Should Lulu, in the calm aftermath, wonder whether she might have been at least partly responsible for the evil suggestion?

10. John, aged 13, went to boarding school. An older boy "went over" him with his hands. John had never experienced any sexual urges before, and did not ex-

perience any now. In his ignorance (not innocence!) he got the idea that this older boy must be an agent of the school doctor. Yet he was vaguely uneasy. Thinking it over worried him and he consulted a priest. (This happened!)

Could such a thing happen to your boy? Had his parents told him to "come up fighting" if any companion attempted such a thing, would John have been saved this serious experience? Though, as a matter of fact, no evil came of it, so far as John was concerned, could his purity have been endangered for life?

QUESTIONS AND DISCUSSION AIDS

1. List the dangers which, from your own experience, you think are to be met in each of these places: schools, nursing homes, factories, offices, dance halls, taverns, military camps, etc. Discuss methods of warning an adolescent of them a) seriously, and b) without creating neurotic fears.

2. Try to phrase for each age level simple warnings concerning the venereal diseases. Discuss methods of inculcating hygienic habits in public lavatories.

3. What dangers in personal immodesty do you think your children might meet? In immodesty with others, playmates, elders?

4. What are the chief arguments against purity which are circulating among teen-agers? (*"Everybody does it." "It's all right if you are in love with the girl." "Try things out first before you get married,"* etc.) Are these arguments dangers in themselves? How can you refute them?

5. What discussions are going the rounds about the premarital use of contraceptives? How can you face this danger?

6. Is your own home safe for your children? Do you get the scandal newspapers? What kinds of books, magazines and papers are lying around? What about the comic books your children are reading? Are all reasonable pro-

prieties observed between your sons and daughters?

7. As a result of this section on warnings, will you suspect every stranger who smiles or talks to your baby? On the other hand, do you think it unfortunate that your child is not more friendly with everyone? Is there room for a common-sense middle course here?

Chapter XIII

Remote Preparation for Marriage

Mature attitudes toward marriage are recognized to be a modern need. Indeed, many secular universities have been so impressed by the fact that they have introduced both regular and extension courses on marriage and family life (for example, the University of California has a course, "Youth and Marriage Today," in University Extension). The need is great because there is so little evidence of family life in modern culture;[1] and few people really consider marriage an institution for the begetting and raising of children, though they may pay lip service to that ideal. At the present time, the concept of marriage is concentrated on "romantic love," physical beauty, sexual attraction, and emotional appeal, which elements are featured in magazines, movies, radio and stage plays. For women, marriage is placed in opposition to a "career," as though motherhood were not a really worthwhile calling.

In generations past, there was no need for special emphasis on marriage and family life. Even though their ideas may occasionally have been erroneous, parents knew family life, practiced it, and passed it along to their children. On their side, children experienced family life and were prepared by such living to found their own families. In our age, the "small" family, and the tremendous (conscious or unconscious) propaganda against the meaning of marriage, has destroyed this

---

1. Cf. Sorokin, Pitirim A., *The Crisis of Our Age* (Dutton, New York, 1941), chapter V.

older education; and even many Catholics, though they live (at times unwillingly) under Catholic principles, have unconsciously accepted these false attitudes. Therefore, today there is a special need of preparation for marriage, and indeed it is high time our Catholic schools and colleges also took up this important work.[2] All Catholic children need a mature and Christian attitude toward marriage.

FOR WHOM?

Most of your children will marry, and even those who will choose the celibate life should do so freely, after at least considering marriage. They can neither marry in a holy manner, nor sacrifice this holy state for the more holy one of consecrated virginity, unless they value matrimony as adult Christians should. In addition, it is our contention that even those of either sex who will surely become religious or priests should have this full formation in the home. In the first place, unless they become contemplatives, a large part of their lives will be spent in advising married people and in protecting the family. If they teach, they must educate by far the greater majority of their pupils for a solid family life. Therefore, it should not be left to their advanced education to give religious and priests an appreciation of the true value of Christian marriage. This they should have from their earliest years.[3]

WHAT FORMATION?

Large portions of this book have been concerned with proper attitudes and remote preparation for marriage;

---

2. Cf. Walsh, George A., "The Religious Need of Modern Youth: Marriage Preparation," in the *Catholic High School Quarterly Bulletin, IV* (April, 1946), pp. 3-5. Since this chapter was written, a number of fine high school programs have come to the attention of the author; *e. g.,* Sister M. Annetta's *The Christian Family Living Series,* W. H. Sadlier Inc., New York, 1952. Excellent courses are now given in most Catholic colleges and good texts are available from a number of Catholic publishers.
3. Cf. encyclical, *On Christian Marriage.*

for example, Chapter V, pp. 48ff., Vocations; Chapter IX, pp. 108ff., Emotional Attitudes toward Body, Marriage, Parenthood. Here we shall add a few other things which young people should know and realize thoroughly as a remote preparation for possible marriage.

DIVORCE

At the turn of the century it was unusual to have even a single acquaintance who was divorced. Now there is scarcely a locality in which a person can live without meeting several divorced people. Our divorce rate has soared until there is now one new divorce for every three new marriages, and the rate shows little sign of any notable decline.

Young people should not take this state of affairs for granted. They must learn that, though a separation may be allowed for a good reason (and with the permission of the bishop), the divorce of persons truly married, giving them freedom to remarry, is against God's law for all. Christ said: "What God has joined together, let no man put asunder" (*Matt.* 19:6). The Church is waging a lone and almost losing battle for this divine law. Simply, validly married people who divorce and "remarry" *are not married.* Though their consciences may not bother them, objectively and really they are living in adulterous unions, and pleasing phrases should not be allowed to cover up this sad state of affairs. ("Mr. and Mrs. So-and-so were married yesterday after recent divorces"; or, "Married: John S. and Mary D., at Reno, she for the third, he for the fourth time." *Married?*) Let adolescents learn to judge these adulterous unions for what they are.

Try also to prevent in your children any tendency to worship Hollywood stars. If they like the acting of an individual and can separate that aspect from his personal life, no harm will be done. Yet the "lives and loves" (very many loves!) of some Hollywood stars are held up as models to our young people, though very few such "lives and loves" will bear close examination, much less imitation. This may apply even to some nominally Catholic stars. Therefore, insist that your children judge this public scandal in its true light. Silence on these subjects is criminal!

This same clear gaze must be turned toward the unions of Catholics who go through ceremonies before a minister or justice of the peace. The statement, "In the eyes of the Church they are not married," should not mean (as it does to some Catholics) that the Church merely withholds its blessing from what is in fact a real marriage. For Catholics, the eyes of the Church are the eyes of God. Catholics who attempt such civil unions are as much in a state of sin as Catholics who live together without a ceremony of any kind. This may seem strong language, but it is nevertheless the truth, and it should be known by all, to counteract the effect of the loose talk, and even looser thinking, of some Catholics. If our adolescents live in the midst of such thinking, with little or no counter-education at home, can we be surprised if they should ignore clear warnings from the pulpit and Catholic school?

BIRTH CONTROL

What Chesterton called "no birth and less control," is a very popular subject for conversation and dispute. In spite of this, many Catholic parents hesitate to mention it. We admit it would be better if it could be ignored, but silence leaves the field open to the advocates of this pernicious thing. There is, of course, no need to indicate to adolescents the methods of contraception. They should, however, know that it is intrinsically evil and never allowed for any reason whatsoever. Let them clearly understand Pius XI (encyclical *On Christian Marriage*):

> Since, therefore, the conjugal act is destined primarily by nature for the begetting of children, those who in exercising it deliberately frustrate its natural power and pur-

pose sin against nature and commit a deed which is shameful and intrinsically vicious.

Mere argument is not enough to prevent this sin in the marriages of your children, for we live in an age which does not reason but acts on "feeling." If, however, children are imbued with a love of marriage as a vocation, if they love children, if they feel the desire to raise up lovers of God, if they want to increase the Mystical Body of Christ on earth, the attacks of pagans will hardly touch them. Indeed, against these ideas what motives can the pagans offer? They argue that parents should be free from the burden of children; that carrying a child causes loss of "figure"; that the economic sacrifice of raising a family is too difficult; that the health of a mother is destroyed by childbearing. To these selfish arguments, they add the pressure of cynical laughter, which is often the most effective of all since most people fear to appear foolish in the eyes of others, no matter how wrong those others may be.

Now, freedom *from* children is hardly a blessing for a married couple. Freedom *for* what? Golf and bridge? Children give purpose and aim to an otherwise aimless life. Economic sacrifices are real, indeed, but more than repaid by the joy of loving children, who are certainly worth every sigh. Again, the argument from health tricks many into sin although, generally speaking, childbearing is physically beneficial and refusal of motherhood is both mentally and physically harmful to most married women.[4] The few cases in which this is not true can be handled by continence, whether absolute or periodic. The rest of the arguments and pressures should be beneath the notice of any reasonable person, and certainly of no value for a militant Catholic.

As a last word against birth control, remind your children that, once chosen, marriage is the vocation or

---

4. Cf. McCann, Frederick John, *Contraception: A Common Cause of Disease* (Central Bureau Press, St. Louis, 1946), pp. 34-38.

means by which they must get to Heaven. A man and wife who continually live in the state of mortal sin, cannot hope for the blessing of God on themselves or on their family, and hence cannot reach Heaven. Nor can they urge that they are so much "in love" that they cannot refrain from this sin. A true lover could never ask his beloved to go to Hell with him!

FAMILY LIFE

Divorce, invalid marriages, contraception, are evils which must be attacked; but even more important than this warfare against the family's foes is the positive inculcation of family living. This depends chiefly on parental example. Thus, parents should show their mutual need of each other and their satisfaction in being together. Actually, it may be helpful at times to point out what each does for the family, lest the children come to take things for granted. For instance, if for any reason one parent is absent because of sickness or business, drive the lesson home by pointing out the void that is left while he or she is necessarily absent.

Give children duties to perform in the family circle. A happy, busy, useful home life teaches children more of family life than they will ever learn from books.[5] All the girls should have an opportunity to cook, sew, wash, iron, clean, and plan home decoration. The boys, too, should learn to contribute. Let them help with repair jobs, painting, washing and drying dishes, etc. It is a sad commentary on home life when we must teach cooking (even fundamentals like boiling eggs) and elementary carpentry in school!

There is no better way of learning the true nature of marriage than a study, or at least a reading, of Pius XI's encyclical *On Christian Marriage,* already cited so often. If this seems too heavy for adolescents, we sug-

---

5. Cf. "Family with Nine Kids," in the *Ladies' Home Journal,* March and April, 1946.

gest the correspondence course *"This Is a Great Sacrament,"* the first ten lessons of which can be had by anyone 17 years of age or older.[6]

BOY MEETS GIRL

Early in adolescence boys and girls will begin to show interest in each other. This can and should be an innocent and joyful discovery of the different nature of each sex and how it complements the other. Young people can learn about the real qualities of men and women, and real living, and by so doing, they are remotely preparing for marriage. Therefore, let them invite their friends home. If you have trained your children well, they will choose only morally decent companions, and will never bring home anyone of whom they need be ashamed. Do not object that your home is too small. We know of a family with eleven children in a six-room house which always manages to have its parlor free for the children's friends! Again, if you have a cellar, get the youngsters to whitewash it, paint the floor, etc., and let them dig up an old record player. Youths are seldom critical of furnishings and they will learn how to enjoy themselves at a minimum of expense. By these means you will provide your adolescents with a safe place in which to grow; and your occasional presence (never suspicious!) will be a reasonable check on any dangerous tendencies.

Steadies

There is one particular danger in modern youth activities, and this is the too early pairing off. If "going steady" merely means that your daughter is sure of an escort every Friday night to a dance, there is little danger. But danger does arise when this pairing off takes

---

6. Published by the Catholic Centre, Ottawa University, 1 Stewart Street, Ottawa 2, Canada.

on the aspect of real company-keeping with a view to marriage. If, as an example, a girl of 17 goes out almost every night for a month or more with the same person and spends most of the evenings alone with him without any real hope of marrying, she needs considerable counsel. In the face of popular adolescent approval of such customs, it is hard to oppose it. First use roundabout reasons: neglect of study, lack of sleep, the missing of so many other interesting persons, etc. If no change is shown, forbid the "going steady." Why? Because it is a mortal sin to indulge in *real* company-keeping without intending to marry or without being able to consider marriage for a long time.[7] Surely it is dangerous to purity for two people who are attracted to each other to be continually and frequently alone together. To enter into such an occasion of sin without a sufficient reason, is sinful in itself.

Company-keeping

Company-keeping can be said to start when a young man and woman begin to pair off with the idea of finding out whether they could make a success of marriage together. Those keeping company have no more "rights" to immodest actions than any other unmarried people, and they must safeguard themselves against the temptations to which their growing attraction may give rise. For this reason, too long a period of courtship should be avoided. Yet what might be "too long" in any one case is difficult to determine. A good norm, *aside from particular circumstances,* is this: real courtship should not last less than six months (so they can really learn to know each other) nor more than a year. Parents still have duties in this matter! A simple warning, caution, etc., will, however, frequently have to suffice. Since these children have grown nearly to maturity, they will

---

7. Cf. Aertnys-Damen, *op. cit.,* II, # 519.

resent interference, and indirect methods will perhaps be most effective.

QUALITIES OF FUTURE PARTNER

Long before an engagement, the qualities of a future partner should be taken into consideration. What are they?

Religion

Catholics are forbidden to marry non-Catholics except for very grave reasons and then only when there is no danger to the Faith of the Catholic party, and when there is certainty that all the children will be baptized and raised as Catholics.[8] This law forbidding mixed marriages can be dispensed with for only a few reasons. The only good reasons which are found in ordinary cases are these: for the woman, that she is past the age when she is likely to have another chance; for either, that it is difficult to find a Catholic partner or there is real hope of conversion of the non-Catholic party. There are indeed other reasons, but they are rarely found (for example, the situation of a widow with children). True, the Church gives dispensations more frequently than the presence of legitimate reasons might indicate, but the parties themselves cannot use her reasons. Briefly, the Church often dispenses for fear that if she does not, the parties will contract a civil marriage and live together in sin! Consequently, because it is wrong to demand a dispensation without a good reason (being "in love" is not of itself a good reason), it is wrong to begin real company-keeping with a view to marriage without *at that time* having a reason for a dispensation.[9] If it is a mortal sin to do this, it is the duty of Catholics to make sure they have contacts among Catholics, and to avoid romantic attach-

---

8. Cf. Code of Canon Law, Canons 1060, 1061, 1070.
9. Cf. Aertnys-Damen, *loc. cit.*

ments to non-Catholics. St. Paul says: "Do not bear the yoke [of marriage] with unbelievers" (*2 Cor.* 6:14). Though this had reference at the time to marriages with pagans, it is still generally applicable to all mixed marriages.

Aside from the Church's prohibition, the facts themselves show that mixed marriages usually do not work, and always are a hazard. Many non-Catholics are beginning to see that two people cannot make a success of life if their major interest, their religion, is different.[10] In a survey reported in *Newsweek,*[11] Dr. Leiffer, a Methodist, states: ". . . in numerous families the tension [of religious difference] continued to be acute even after twenty years of marriage." Such an argument is only from the vantage point of temporal happiness— how much more forceful the argument from that of eternal happiness! There cannot be true spiritual unity of husband and wife when the non-Catholic party does not believe in or participate in the religion of his spouse, the Catholic home practices, education of the children, First Communion, Confirmation, etc. Something will always be lacking, for the non-Catholic will feel "left out," and the family will miss his active participation. Furthermore, no non-Catholic sect prohibits divorce or birth control. How can there be complete giving of each other, or real moral agreement, if there is disagreement on these two fundamental matters? Lest any non-Catholic partner in mixed marriage take all this as a mere personal affront, let us ask this question: "Granting you have made a reasonable success of your marriage, is it not true that religious differences have made it difficult for you to obtain perfect marital union of mind and heart with your spouse?" We are convinced that your answer must be, "Yes, it has been difficult."

From all this it should be clear that it is the seri-

---

10. Cf. Adams-Packard, *How To Pick a Mate* (Dutton, New York, 1946), pp. 139-146; Evelyn Millis Duval, *Building Your Marriage* (Public Affairs Pamphlet No. 113, Public Affairs Committee, New York, 1946).
11. January 31, 1949, p. 64. Quoted with permission of the publisher.

ous duty of Catholic parents to instill in their children the obligation of choosing a Catholic partner in marriage. It should be a fundamental ideal for Catholic young people. In looking forward to marriage, no other possibility should be envisioned.[12]

Moral Character

Imbue your children with the idea of choosing as a marriage partner a person of upright morality, for few succeed in reforming their partners after the wedding ceremony. This is especially true regarding sexual sins, drunkenness or dishonesty. If either or both partners have sinned habitually in these ways, it is unlikely that immoral conduct will be avoided during or even in marriage. This is another reason for caution during company-keeping. If the future partners cannot keep chaste before marriage, they will hardly keep chaste in marriage. This is not merely a Catholic opinion. Non-Catholic studies have indicated that a breakdown of chastity before marriage leads to mutual contempt, suspicion and mistrust; and surely a marriage cannot last long if suspicion holds sway.

Compatibility

Future spouses should have similar likes and dislikes over a wide field, but not necessarily identical interests, for this would make a dull life. Compatibility means that they have the same ideas of what is right, proper, polite, etc., and that all their interests *fit* reasonably together. This holds for wealth level, intellectual level, and so on. Though stories of successful marriages between rich and poor, intelligent and mediocre, refined and brusque, are frequent, the actual

---

12. Cf. Lord, Daniel A., S. J., *Marry Your Own,* The Queen's Work, St. Louis; Carroll, T., *Mixing Your Marriage?* Liturgical Press, Collegeville, Minn.; Miller, D. F., *Can Mixed Marriages Be Happy?* Liguorian Pamphlets, Liguori, Mo.

chances of success in these cases are low. "Marry your own" is a worthwhile motto in every sphere.

Maturity

Physical maturity is naturally expected in those who marry, but mental and emotional maturity is equally needed and less often possessed. Many modern works have pointed out that emotional immaturity is almost a characteristic of the American nation.[13] Now, unless two people are adult in their approach to reality, they will find it difficult, if not impossible, to make a success of marriage. Sulking, childish traits, lack of decisiveness, inability to give and take, wreck many marriages. One of the best tests for maturity is this: Can a person make clear, considered decisions, carry them out, and take the consequences without excessive fear or worry, whether the outcome is good or bad? The answer must be, "Yes," before one can rate a person mature.

Physical Fitness

Physical fitness is frequently denied consideration, despite the fact that many marriages are unhappy *as* a result. By physical fitness is meant normal robustness of body to bear the burdens of family demands. This does not mean that athletes alone may safely marry, nor that the unhealthy must not marry. It means that each one must weigh the matter well before deciding on marriage with one not normally healthy. It means that a young man should ask himself whether he is equal to the task of supporting a family, and a young woman should ask herself whether she can bear children without great danger. They must also discuss these questions with each other. If they agree to marry, despite

---

13. Cf. Strecker, Edward A., *Their Mother? Sons,* J. B. Lippincott, New York, 1946; "What's Wrong with American Mothers?" in the *Saturday Evening Post,* October 26, 1946; "The American Character," in *Life Magazine,* August 18, 1947.

adverse indications, at least let them have their eyes wide open to the *sacrifices for life* that such disabilities may entail. One of the sacrifices demanded might be the practice of continence for long periods.

Physical Attraction

The modern mind places this quality first and considers that unless two people violently desire each other, they make a mistake in marrying. But in fact physical desire is the least important element, for a successful marriage must be built on deeper foundations than attraction of body. As long as persons are not repelled by each other, their physical attraction can usually be developed to meet all the demands of marriage. Physical attraction is important, of course, and that there should be some desire. Yet, if marriage is based on this sole qualification, it is doomed to failure. "A marriage based on sex attraction alone carries in itself, from the beginning, the germ of destruction," says Allers.[14] This is easily seen when we recall that sex satisfaction is essentially selfish; it is a "getting." A marriage based on sexual pleasure cannot endure because real marriage is a "giving," not a "getting," and it is only in giving that the partners may hope for a return.

Parents must give their children an eye for the right qualities in a prospective marriage partner. As in all education, they can do this best by giving the example of their own happiness in marriage. Secondly, parents should teach their children to come to them for advice; and this, in turn, must be given cautiously, with an effort to make them judge correctly for themselves. Try to judge, and help your sons and daughters to judge, the person concerned *objectively*. Point out the faults and difficulties, but let them make the decision. In discussing such matters, try to eliminate a mere

---

14. *Sex Psychology in Education* (Herder, St. Louis, 1937), p. 259. Quoted with permission of the publisher.

dislike or bias and prejudice which has no real foundation. Tone of voice, color of hair, manner of dress, origin outside of one's "set," etc., make no difference unless these indicate some other more basic and objectionable trait.

QUESTIONS AND DISCUSSION AIDS

1. Should there be many more courses on marriage and family life in our Catholic high schools and colleges? Are the Popes' condemnations of sex instruction in public against this? What might some of the courses include? Do you believe it is true that past generations learned these things without formal instruction? What do you think of the statement that *all* should have mature attitudes on marriage?

2. Do you find that your thinking on divorce and "remarriage" has slipped into a pagan groove? Discuss some of the recent arguments for birth control which you have heard. Will it not be even harder for the next generation (your children) to withstand such propaganda? What can you do about it? About the conditions that make the arguments seem plausible?

3. Is there real family life in your home? Or is your home merely a hotel, a place to sleep and eat? Does your family have frequent recreation together? Discuss methods by which each family member can make contributions to home life. Have you *ever* read anything on Christian marriage and family life? Would it make any difference in your education if you had? May we suggest some material?[15]

4. Discuss methods of control in boy-girl relationships without dampening them. Do you have the problem of "steadies" with your adolescents? What is their mind on this matter? How can you control this indirectly? When would you make a positive prohibition?

5. What is company-keeping? Are any "liberties" allowed?

---

15. For example, the encyclical *On Christian Marriage;* also *Life Together,* by Wingfield Hope, Sheed and Ward, 1944.

What means can young people use to remain chaste? How can you teach those means to your children without seeming to intrude? Discuss what might be a too long courtship. Give examples.

6. Do you believe that falling in love is something over which one has no control? Is the question, "What kind of father (or mother) will he (or she) make for my children?" in any way improper? Would some people consider it so? Why? Is it not a healthier approach than questions of glamour and bodily beauty? Do you think that young people fall in love today too easily?

7. What is wrong with a mixed marriage? Did you know it was sinful to keep company with a non-Catholic without a reason for a dispensation? Do your children know? Do you realize how unflattering is the reason for many of the dispensations granted? (That is, fear that the couple will merely go through a civil ceremony and live together.) Have you ever heard St. Paul's prohibition before? Do you think the fundamental difference of opinion on divorce and birth control is a source of much unhappiness and sin in mixed marriages?

8. Do you believe people change their characters in marriage? Can you recall any examples of individuals who have not "changed their spots" despite the fond hopes of their spouses? Is it possible, on the contrary, to progress in virtue together?

9. List some common interests that bind marriages more firmly; some interests which tend to break them. (Are you a golf-widow; a bridge-widower?) How might people help overcome these problems?

10. What is maturity? What is a good yardstick for it? Do you agree that there are many childish personalities walking about in adult bodies? How would you help your children grow to emotional maturity? (*Demand that they make decisions. Refuse to protect them from the consequences of their acts. Give them responsibilities according to their age and hold them strictly accountable. Allow them a reasonable field for freedom of choice—clothes, recreation, study-time.*)

11. Is it true that sexual desire is essentially selfish? Can you think of any young couples who are successfully and happily married though they seem to lack worldly "sex appeal"?

12. What is advice? Is it "telling people what to do"? Or is it helping them to decide for themselves? Do your children come to you for advice? Why or why not? If they do not ask help, could it be that you are no longer a close friend?

Chapter XIV

Immediate Preparation for Marriage

Once a couple has agreed on marriage, and if any impediments exist they have been cared for, there are still some points on which a son or daughter should be instructed by a parent.[1]

MARRIAGE RIGHTS

It is not enough for a young couple to enter marriage with a mere knowledge of the fact of marital intercourse. They should also be instructed in sufficient time about their practical sexual adjustments in marriage. Though by no means the most important consideration in marriage, a satisfactory sexual life is one important basis for marital happiness. It is unfortunate that some think this matter comes by instinct. There are, indeed, urges of instinct; but methods in this as in all matters can be learned in but two ways, either by experience or by instruction. The first is hazardous because a brutal first experience may be the ultimate cause of marital disaster. Such disillusioning experience could be caused by so little a thing as forgetting the different rapidity of sexual reaction in the

---

1. We omit a discussion of impediments to matrimony because these can easily be found elsewhere (for example, Connell, Francis J., C.SS.R., *Matrimony*, Paulist Press, New York, 1940). The parish priest, whom the couple should consult at least a month before the ceremony, will discuss the possible impediments in the so-called "pre-marital investigation."

two sexes. Therefore it would seem that some instruction is necessary.

A couple can obtain their information from a wholesome or an unwholesome source. Now, parents are, or should be, a wholesome source, but if they do not give this necessary help, the young persons will be driven to ask advice from possibly erroneous or even sinful sources. From these they may learn "rather the art of sinning in a subtle way than the virtue of living chastely" (encyclical *On Christian Marriage*). It is imperative, then, that the father (or perhaps an elder married brother) give this proper instruction to the bridegroom, and the mother or an elder married sister to the young bride, even though such intimate instruction might seem most embarrassing. If parents cannot or will not give this information, they should at least send the young persons to a Catholic doctor or nurse.

In Person or Booklet?

Some think that a booklet would be better since it lends itself to calm reading and repetition. Its very impersonality precludes too much danger of sin (remember that the morality for the unmarried binds engaged people). Others think that personal instruction is better, since, if it is given simply and reverently, reverent attitudes will be adopted from the attitude of the adviser. It is difficult to arrive at a decision. It seems to make little difference as long as the facts are learned in a proper emotional atmosphere. If a booklet is decided on, one can usually be obtained from a doctor or marriage counselor.

How Much Information?

There is no need for tremendous detail or a vivid description of sexual pleasure. Marital intimacies are attractive enough in themselves, unless early training has made them seem disgusting or shameful. The instruction should be sufficient to indicate what to expect, yet not so detailed as to give a formula or blueprint which is to be unvaried in its use. There is no need for anyone to live this or any other department of his life "by the book," and some joy of discovery and spontaneity should be left to the couple. Nevertheless, enough must be explained to allow the young couple to approach their first sexual experience calmly and with some measure of confidence and knowledge. Each partner should know well *what is expected by, and what to expect of, the other.* Above all, each should learn consideration for the different nature of the opposite sex (the male, passionate and active; the female, slow of response, demanding loving acts, etc.). It may also be well to add that physical delight cannot be expected to be perfect at the first encounter. In this and other spheres, marriage is a process of lifelong learning. A couple will need time for perfect adjustment in both bodily and spiritual spheres.

When?

Some say that detailed physical information should not precede marriage by more than one or two days. On the other hand, since a modern marriage does not seem a leisurely thing, and the last few days are one flurry of external preparation, it seems sensible to give the information earlier. Information given a week or two before will enable the spouses to accustom themselves to the ideas, and to become calm about them. Obviously this information should be given in private, and never to both parties together. If any doubts arise concerning the morality of this instruction, apply the moral principles for modesty as listed in Chapter VIII, that is: though information of this nature is stimulating to the passions, there is a necessary reason for knowing the simple facts; one may, therefore, legitimately acquire this knowledge while being careful not to consent to any physical pleasure which might arise involuntarily.

More Physiology?

A more complete physiology may be very useful to the couple at this time, though not absolutely necessary. Perhaps this can be better left to their early married life. Many young married people are curious as to what goes on within them especially during pregnancy. They have every right to know if they wish. Yet there is danger in procuring many of the secular books advertised, for some are coarse or even immoral. At the very least, most books will have one chapter approving contraception. Fortunately there are a number of good Catholic texts which will provide this information. Parents may encourage the young couple to complete the final chapters of "This Is a Great Sacrament." A new text for the use of individuals, couples, or groups has been issued by the Family Life Bureau of the National Catholic Welfare Conference. Entitled *Together in Christ,* it is also available as a correspondence course. Other Catholic works suitable for use in pre-marital instruction are listed in the bibliography.

SEX MORALITY FOR THE MARRIED

Chastity (remember our definition?) is still to be observed in marriage, though it has different principles of application, which are as follows:

1. Since marriage is a contract, and the contract is concerned with acts of procreation, *each party has equal rights to the marriage act.* To refuse the other his marital rights, except for a serious reason (for example, sickness, danger of miscarriage, etc.) is a mortal sin. When in doubt, a confessor should be consulted.

2. Neither may stimulate himself or partner to full satisfaction out of connection with a properly completed

marriage act.

3. Birth control (a popular and false name for contraception or Onanism) is always a serious sin, which no reason whatsoever will justify.*

4. Continence, whether periodic (the so-called "Rhythm") or total, may be practiced under the following definite conditions: a) The practice must be freely undertaken by *mutual* consent; b) There must be no serious danger of unchastity or loss of conjugal love in either party as a result of the practice; c) There must be a positive and good reason for adopting the practice. The presence or absence of these conditions should be decided with the help of a confessor.[2]

5. No sexual thought or desire may be deliberately directed to a third person without serious sin.

6. All else which is reasonable and agreeable to both persons, is allowed. Thoughts, desires, kisses and embraces, though rightly considered immodest before marriage, are allowable so long as none of the above principles are violated (especially the second).

ACT OF VIRTUE—WHAT IS RIGHT

It may be well to note again that marital acts between spouses in accordance with the above principles are virtuous! The virtue of justice is exercised in giving a partner his rights. The virtue of chastity is exercised in using sexual acts according to God's law. The virtue of love is exercised in making these acts expressions of love. If the partner is really loved supernaturally, that is, *in* and *for* God, the act is one of supernatural charity. If the partners are in the state of grace and acting with proper intention, their acts are supernaturally meritorious. It is obvious therefore, that there is no impropriety in going to Communion

---

2. Cf. Aertnys-Damen, *op. cit.,* II, # 897.
* In addition, today's birth control pills, implants and shots often work by causing a very early *abortion,* even if the woman is not aware that this is happening. (Also, the IUD operates by causing a very early abortion.) —*Publisher,* 2003.

after the use of the marriage rights. If the act is not sinful in any way, if it is indeed virtuous, it cannot be out of place to approach the Holy Table afterward.

RESTRAINT

Despite the clear truths stated above, there is danger that the marriage act will be performed for mere animal pleasure, and result in excess and abuse. Just as pleasures of taste may be abused by overindulgence, so may legitimate sexual pleasures. Surely marriage is no place for sexual orgies, and nature herself penalizes for overindulgence in the sexual as in the other appetites. Excess will dull the mind, make it unfit for nobler pursuits (for example, thought, prayer, love on a higher plane), and will even kill the sexual pleasures themselves. Also, too frequent sex satisfaction but whets the appetite and makes continence (when and if necessary) exceedingly difficult to practice. Therefore,

> . . . Let husband and wife resolve: . . . to use the rights given them by marriage in a way that will always be Christian and sacred, more especially in the first years of wedlock, so that should there be need of continence afterward, custom will have made it easier for each to preserve it (encyclical *On Christian Marriage*).

Many occasions will arise demanding restraint and continence. Indeed, from time to time as much self-control is needed in marriage as before; for once an individual learns sexual delight, it is hard to remain continent at various necessary times. For instance, before and after childbirth, continence is imperative. Again, business trips which cause a necessary separation, long serious illness, and other occasions may demand prolonged self-control. Unless the spouses have practiced restraint, they will find it difficult, if not impossible, to observe this continence. Remember that a sin during this time adds the malice of *unfaithfulness* to the impurity committed.

Christian Asceticism

Modern writers stress the beauty and goodness of the marital act, and this is as it should be. Yet some Catholics have followed suit to such a degree that there is danger of losing the ideal of Christian asceticism, since there is room for Christian asceticism in this as in every pleasure (and other pleasures are *good* too!). Let St. Paul give the norm (*1 Cor.* 7:5):

Do not deprive each other [of marital pleasures], except perhaps by consent, for a time, that you may give yourselves to prayer; and return together again lest Satan tempt you because you lack self-control.

Such asceticism will engender self-control, prevent brutish excess, and make a Christian life more holy. During times of penance (Lent, Advent), such abstinence might well be used by the spouses to declare before God that they do not "give themselves to their lust" (*Tob.* 6:17), but exercise their rights and accept the joy that ensues, out of love of God, His law, children, and each other. Note, however, St. Paul's conditions, "by consent," "for a time," and the reason—a spiritual one! Neither partner may adopt an "ascetical" restraint at the expense of the other or for a selfish reason. What might be excess, or in what an acceptable Christian asceticism might consist, must be decided by the spouses *together.*

MISCARRIAGE

The young married couple should be taught what to do in case of a miscarriage. Since it is possible that a living soul is there, conditional Baptism should be conferred by husband or wife in the following manner: if the fetus can be found, the sac in which it is encased should be slit and the whole dipped up and down in warm water while saying the words: "If thou art living, I baptize thee in the name of the Father and of the Son, and of the Holy Ghost." The aborted fetus should be buried in consecrated ground, a task which, in a Catholic hospital, is always carried out. In other cases the parents should get in touch with a Catholic undertaker. (Cf. Healy, Mary Lanigan, *Baby in a Shoe Box,* Catholic Information Society, New York.)*

ABORTION—STERILIZATION

In modern life one can hardly avoid the propaganda for these two crimes. First, therefore, the couple should know that directly to bring about abortion is equivalent to murder and is punished by excommunication from the Church.[3] Secondly, sterilization or whatever is equivalent (severing any organ, etc.), is never allowed except for the good of the body as such (for example, when the organ is diseased). Fear of difficult pregnancy is not a sufficient reason. Thus, any doctor's demand for an operation during pregnancy, or for sterilization of any kind, should always be referred to a priest for a moral (not medical) decision. The matter is too involved to discuss here, though a Catholic doctor or any doctor practicing in a Catholic hospital usually knows what is permissible in such cases.*

Though what has gone before should be known by every newlywed, how much can be successfully given by parents is a question. Perhaps giving them this brief chapter to read would suffice for general moral cases, while the practical physical adjustments can be indicated separately by the parent or some other qualified person, or by a booklet.

Please note that the last two chapters of this work, though brief, are packed with very important material. Each sentence could have been expanded to a para-

---

3. Code of Canon Law, 2350, § 1.
* Unfortunately, today many Catholic doctors, hospitals and priests cannot be relied upon to uphold the Church's teaching on medical-moral questions; a Catholic must make sure that the one he consults is orthodox.—*Editor,* 1993.

graph, each paragraph to a chapter, and a whole book would scarcely do justice to these and some other points space limitations have forced us to omit. Consider these two chapters, then, as a *minimum outline* of the remote and proximate preparations for marriage. Certainly, they are the absolute minimum to be expected from Catholic parents.

QUESTIONS AND DISCUSSION AIDS

1. Did you receive any practical instruction before your wedding? Discuss the difficulties that young married people have because they do not get such instruction. Would even the most vague instruction be better than none? Who, in your opinion, can best give this information with the least emotional disturbance on both sides?

2. Do you think people learn anything of a practical nature from mere instinct (without any experience or instruction)? On the other hand, haven't you seen booklets for young married people which pretend to help them in marital adjustments but which you know are erroneous? Could you bring yourself to give this instruction simply and reverently? Would you prefer to give the young person a booklet and thus wash your hands of a delicate matter? Why?

3. How soon should the spouses be instructed before marriage? Would the evening before be a time of calm instruction? Is people's wonder about the physical processes within them, legitimate curiosity?

4. Were you instructed in the morality given here? If not, would such instruction have helped you? Do you think you have any obligation to take needless worry from your children who are soon to marry? Is there any impropriety in going to the Sacraments after satisfying marital obligations?

5. What virtues are exercised in performing marital acts in a holy manner? Did you ever think of them in that light before?

6. Why is restraint and self-control necessary? Are there not many occasions for necessary self-control in married life?

7. Did you know how to baptize in case of a miscarriage? Explain why it is important in this sad case.

8. Did you know that all who contribute to a direct abortion are excommunicated? Why do you think the Church is so severe in this matter? Do you think you could give the necessary moral instruction to a young person about to be married? If not, how would you remedy this lack?

Conclusion

Parents, the many pages you have studied may seem long and complex. At one time the author had all the information compressed into forty pages, but he felt that many phases would be overlooked if it were published in so brief a form. Time and space have been given to some points, not so much because the meaning demanded it, but simply to make certain that you would *think* about them daily as Catholics. The subject is not by nature very complex; but it is most important that you *absorb* the principles—that is, take them in so deeply that they are there unconsciously, to be used without effort. You are not asked to attempt memorizing a schematic outline of the whole. However, do memorize, in any of the forms given, the Four Moral Principles for the unmarried. Memorize also the "facts of life" and some of the simpler ways of stating them. With these in your memory, and a healthy attitude developed by the study of this work, you will be capable of giving sex education. Then you need refer to this work (or others following it) only in case of a special problem. For example, if a son or daughter is about to be married, that will necessitate your rereading the last two chapters.

After spending so many weeks on this subject, your mind is naturally filled with it, and perhaps you are now frightened by your responsibilities and your awakened sense of the dangers facing your children. Perhaps you have resolved to campaign for purity in your children. Don't! Let this new knowledge fit in with all the rest that you know of real life. All you need for the duty of sex education or (now that you know better) education for chastity, is *Confidence, Caution* and *Common Sense*. Let these three "C's" be your motto. There has yet to exist a parent, with or without education, who cannot meet his obligations in this matter if only he keeps his feet firmly on real ground. Do not go up in the air with worry; it will only make your task harder.

You may be disappointed that you have been given but one "model of instruction." But the author continues to believe that models are not satisfactory. However, a series of pamphlets for parents on each important point are to follow this work. In the meantime, the annotated list following will supply sufficient models if you need them. Now you are in a position really to judge their value and to select what is helpful.

Bibliographical Note

Throughout this work there have been numerous references to books and pamphlets on sex education. These should give sufficient reading matter on particular points. It seems advisable, however, to include an annotated list of works which may be of additional help. Those marked with a single asterisk are especially worthwhile. Those marked with double asterisks will give *words and methods* of imparting sex knowledge and training. To the author, there seems to be no satisfactory booklet from the Catholic point of view on what to tell the very young child who asks about sexual matters. However, the suggestions in this book should be of assistance until the second book of this series is published.

For Pre-Adolescence

1. ** Bruckner, P. J., *How To Give Sex Instruction*. The Queen's Work, 3115 South Grand Blvd., St. Louis 18, MO, 1937 (P[1] 25c). This text is perhaps the finest available. It gives one instruction for boys and one for girls. It also supplies an outline that may be followed when using your own words. It contains an excellent series of principles. It omits, however, the answers to one or two crucial questions.

2. ** Juergens, Sylvester P., *Fundamental Talks on Purity*. Bruce Publishing Company, 400 North Broadway, Milwaukee 1, WI, 1941 (P 75c). This is a good booklet, but it leans too heavily on the animal kingdom and on physiology. Balanced with Father Bruckner's pamphlet, however, it gives all necessary "facts of life."

---

1. P indicates pamphlet; B indicates book.

221

FOR EARLY ADOLESCENCE

3. ** A Catholic Woman Doctor, *Growing Up: A Book for Girls.* Benziger Bros., 6-8 Barclay St., New York 8, NY, 1946 (P 75c).

4. ** Pire, Lionel E., C. PP. S., *The Heart of a Young Man.* F. Pustet Co., 14 Barclay St., New York 8, NY, 1931 (P 40c).

    These two booklets are longer than the first two mentioned but are well worth reading.

5. ** Meyer, Fulgence, O. F. M., *Helps to Purity.* St. Francis Bookshop, 1618 Vine St., Cincinnati 10, OH, 1929 (B paper, 50c; cloth, $1.00). To be read by the adolescent girl. Despite a slightly stiff style, this booklet is excellent.

6. ** Meyer, Fulgence, O. F. M., *Safeguards of Chastity.* St. Francis Bookshop, 1929 (B paper, 50c; cloth, $1.00). For the adolescent boy. Very good. Same recommendation as for the previous booklet.

7. ** *Mother's Little Helper.*† Franciscan Herald Press, 1434 W. 51st St., Chicago 9, IL, 1952 (P 50c). An instruction in three parts which a mother might use with her daughter. A bit too reserved and stilted, but might give some valuable helps.

8. ** *Listen, Son!*† Franciscan Herald Press, 1952 (P 50c). An instruction in three parts which a father might use as a model in talking with his sons. Excellent in every way.

The above six titles may be given to the adolescent to read if necessary. However, never give children any book on this subject, no matter how well recommended, until you have read it to judge its suitability *for this child.*

FOR YOUNG TEENAGERS (14-16)

9.   Sattler, Henry V., C. SS. R., *The Challenge of Chastity,*

---

† Available from Angelus Press, 2915 Forest Avenue, Kansas City, MO 64109. —*Editor,* 1993.

Liguorian Pamphlets, Liguori, Mo., 1957 (P 10c). A positive presentation of the virtue of chastity.

10. ** Miller, D. F., *How To Say "No" to Boy Friends.* Liguorian Pamphlets, Liguori, MO, 1951 (P 5c). An excellent bit of psychological retort to the question of kissing, petting, etc. Can be given to the teenager to read.

11. Burnite, Alvena, *Tips for Teens,* Bruce Publishing Co., Milwaukee, WI, 1955 (B paper, $1.25) . A smoothly written book that teen-agers will like.

12. Donnelly, Antoinette, *Tips for Teeners.* Catholic Information Society, 214 W. 31st St., New York 1, NY (P 5c).

13. A Teenager, *Teen Talks.* Catholic Information Society (P 5c each):

No. 1—*On Dress;* No. 2—*On Dates;* No. 3—*On Decency;* No. 4—*On Drink;* No. 5—*On Magazines;* No. 6—*On Marriage;* No. 7—*On Movies;* No. 8 —So *You Think You've Grown Up?* Written in racy teen-talk, these eight pamphlets will be very acceptable to teenagers of both sexes, though they will appeal mostly to girls. They employ both emotional and rational approaches.

14. * Kirsch, Felix M., O. F. M. Cap., *Training in Chastity.* Our Sunday Visitor Press, Huntington, Ind., 1951 (P 10c). A good foundation in sexual morality for both sexes.

15. ** Haley, Joseph E., *Accent on Purity,* Fides Publishers, Notre Dame, IN, 1948 (B paper, 95c). This book is an excellent Catholic work on the subject. Its chief virtue is its very positive approach to the matter. The model instructions, however, seem best adapted to more educated people.

FOR OLDER TEENAGERS (17-19)

16. ** Kelly, Gerald, S. J., *Modern Youth and Chastity.* The Queen's Work, St. Louis, MO, 1941 (P 35c). Is with-

out peer in the treatment of sexual morality for both sexes. Gives just about all the answers. Its one defect is that it is written for first-year college men and women, thus making it a bit steep for the ordinary person. It is suitable for those in the last year of high school, but demands study, not mere reading. See footnote, p. 136.—*Editor,* 1993.

17. Popenoe, Paul, *Building Sex into Your Life.* American Institute of Family Relations, 5287 Sunset Blvd., Los Angeles 27, CA. (P 25c). This pamphlet by a non-Catholic is more valuable to parents than to teenagers. It indicates the impact of modern pagan sex propaganda and gives some of the best *natural* answers for chastity. However, never use its arguments alone.

18. Dietz, Francis X., *What Catholic Girls Should Know about Marriage.* Fides Press, Notre Dame, IN, 1960 (B paper, 95c). A text on marriage for high-school girls.

19. Schnepp, A. F., and G. J., *To God through Marriage.* Bruce Publishing Co., Milwaukee, WI, 1957 (B paper, $1.48). A high-school text, mostly along sociological lines.

20. Stanford, Edward V., *Preparing for Marriage.* Mentzer, Bush and Co., 2210 South Parkway, Chicago 16, IL, 1958 (B paper, $1.50). A text for high-school boys.

21. Kelly, George A., *The Catholic Youth's Guide to Life and Love.* Random House, 457 Madison Ave., New York, NY, 1960 (B $3.95). A fine presentation of the evolution of the teenager through dating and courtship.

22. Schmiedeler, Edgar, O. S. B., *Looking toward Marriage.* Family Life Bureau, N. C. W. C., Washington, D. C., 1948 (P 50c). A good high-school text that is now in its fifth edition.

FOR THOSE PREPARING FOR MARRIAGE

23. ** *"This Is a Great Sacrament."* The Catholic Centre, Ottawa University, 1 Stewart St., Ottawa 2, Canada

($7 per individual, $10 per engaged couple; suitable loose-leaf binder container, $1.50). This correspondence course is simple, practical, and inspiring; it covers every angle of marriage from the wedding ceremony to the problem of in-laws.

24. ** Sattler, Henry V., C. SS. R., ed., *Together in Christ: A Preparation for Marriage*. Family Life Bureau, National Catholic Welfare Conference, Washington, D. C., 1960 (B $3.50). This is a series of 11 booklets in a folder for those preparing immediately for marriage. It is for use by groups or individuals, and is also in preparation as a correspondence course.

25. Clarke, William R., O. P., ed., *One in Mind, One in Heart, One in Affections*. Providence College Press, Providence, RI, 1956 (P 50c). A series of lectures to college students preparing for marriage.

26. Cana Conference of Chicago, *Beginning Your Marriage* (P 50c). This pamphlet, treating chiefly the physical adjustments in marriage, is for the soon-to-be-married and is available through your local pastor.

27. Buetow, Harold A., *What Every Bride and Groom Should Know*. Bruce Publishing Co., Milwaukee, WI, 1958 (B paper, $1.25). Contains a fine and understandable preparation for marriage.

28. O'Connor, John, *Preparation for Marriage and Family Life*. Paulist Press, 180 Varick St., New York, NY (P 35c). A study club outline with discussion questions.

29. Kelly, George A., *The Catholic Marriage Manual*. Random House, New York, NY, 1958 (B $4.95). An excellent manual to be used by those preparing for marriage.

It contains a fine chapter by a medical man on the physical relationship.

30. Miller, Donald F., *Pre-Marriage Problems*. Liguorian Pamphlets, Liguori, MO. (P 25c). Presents a solution to most of the moral problems arising during courtship.

31.   Lovasik, Lawrence G., S. V. D., *Clean Love in Courtship.*
       Radio Replies Press, 500 Robert St., St. Paul, MN. (P
       50c). This contains an excellent analysis of the rea-
       sons for pre-marital chastity and the problems inher-
       ent in preserving that chastity.

32.   Meyer, Fulgence, O. F. M., *Plain Talks on Marriage.*
       St. Francis Bookshop, 1927 (B paper, 60c; cloth $1.00).
       A good book but dated in language. Young people usu-
       ally prefer a more modern style.

33.   Hope, Wingfield, *Life Together.* Sheed and Ward, 64
       University Place, New York 3, NY, 1944 (B $2.75). A
       fine, modern treatment of marriage based on Chris-
       tian principles, of particular value for those who need
       to re-Christianize their approach to marriage.

THEORY

34.   * Pius XII, *Guiding Christ's Little Ones.* National Cath-
       olic Welfare Conference, Washington, D. C., 1942 (P
       10c). An address to mothers and teachers. One can
       find in it the complete vindication of Catholic sex
       education.

35.   Sattler, Henry V., C. SS. R., *Educating Parents to Sex
       Instruction.* Liguorian Pamphlets, Liguori, MO, 1957
       (P 25c). Some fresh viewpoints on chastity education
       interwoven in the schematic outline of *Parents, Chil-
       dren and the Facts of Life.*

36.   * Kirsch, Felix M., O. F. M. Cap., *Sex Education and
       Training in Chastity.* Benziger Bros., New York, NY,
       1930. This book, by a pioneer in presenting Catholic
       thought on this subject, is exhaustive in its treat-
       ment, and thus rather heavy for the average reader.
       Though out of print, it is still available in many
       libraries.

37.   * King, J. Leycester, S. J., *Sex Enlightenment and the
       Catholic.* Burns Oates and Washbourne, 28 Ashley
       Pl., London, S. W. 1, England. Out of print, but is to
       be found in libraries. The best rational defense of
       Catholic sex education available, this is brief and

pointed, but exacting reading.

38.   * Allers, Rudolf, *Sex Psychology in Education.* B. Herder Co., 15-17 S. Broadway, St. Louis 2, MO, 1937. Unfortunately out of print. May be obtained in libraries. The finest book of its kind, though rather difficult reading. However, the effort of reading it will be amply repaid.

39.   O'Brien, John A., ed., *Sex-Character Education.* Our Sunday Visitor Press, Huntington, Indiana, 1952 (B paper, $1.50). Father O'Brien here gathers together a number of fine talks on chastity and sex education.

40.   Buckley, Joseph, *Christian Design for Sex.* Fides Publishers, Notre Dame, Indiana, 1952 (B $3.50). Though portions of this work are a little too theological for parents, the material will reward the study.

41.   * Wilkin, Vincent, *The Image of God in Sex.* Sheed and Ward, New York, NY, 1955 (B $1.75). The theological background of sexual differences.

PRACTICE

42.   Odenwald, Robert P., M. D. *How God Made You.* P. J. Kenedy, 12 Barclay St., New York, NY, 1960 (B $2.50). A beautiful picture book which parents can read with younger children.

43.   * Fleege, Urban, *Self-Revelation of the Adolescent Boy.* Bruce Publishing CO, Milwaukee, WI, 1945. Helps toward understanding the problems of the modern boy in every phase of his life. It is a statistical and analytical survey of 2,000 Catholic high school boys. Out of print.

44.   Knoebber, Sister Mildred, 0. S. B., *Self-Revelation of the Adolescent Girl.* Bruce Publishing Co., 1936 (unfortunately out of print; may be found in some libraries). Fleege gives the chief findings as footnotes for comparison with his own.

45.   Mission Helpers, *Vital Steps to Chastity.* Mission

Helpers of the Sacred Heart, Towson, MD, 1960 (P $1.00). Newly revised edition. Though this booklet is designed primarily to give a lesson plan to teachers of each grade from 1 through 12, it is also invaluable for parents.

46.　＊ Lord, Daniel A., S. J., *Some Notes for the Guidance of Parents*. The Queen's Work, St. Louis, MO, 1944 (B paper, $1.50). This book is extremely valuable and should be in every household. It treats many subjects besides sex, and you will find it delightful reading, packed with practical aids. It will enable you to integrate sex education into all your formation of your children.

47.　＊ Lord, Daniel A., S. J., *Some Notes on the Guidance of Youth*. The Queen's Work, 1938 (B paper, $1.25). For youth counselors, but parents will profit equally by reading it. Recommended as highly as No. 46 above.

There are many more good Catholic texts which are not listed, since too many might confuse you. Those marked above with a single asterisk will give you plenty to do. Of those marked with a double asterisk, at least one in each sex-age group (for example, pre-adolescent, adolescent, older adolescent, etc.) should be obtained by your study group.

There are some excellent works by non-Catholics. However, none of them can be recommended entirely, since the approach is natural whereas we live in a supernatural order. Furthermore, many such texts are erroneous on several points, notably on masturbation and (in marriage) on birth prevention. With so much good Catholic literature available, there is no necessity for anyone but a research student to read the other.

For those who would like to give some sex instruction by indirect methods, we suggest the following books. Almost any public library has them:

48.　　Laverty, Maura, *Never No More*. Longmans, Green, 119 W. 40th St., New York, NY, 1942. A beautiful novel about a teenager. Contains the excellent instruction on menstruation already referred to in this book. Out of print, but available in libraries.

49. Daly, Maureen, *Seventeenth Summer.* Dodd, Mead, 432 Park Avenue South, New York, NY, 1942 (B $3.00; illustrated edition, $3.75). This is a fine novel of a first love affair and it indicates some of the temptations to be avoided. Has been reprinted through the years since first being published.

50. Laverty, Maura, *No More Than Human.* Longmans, Green, New York, NY, 1944. The adventures of an 18-year-old girl as a governess in Spain are detailed in this story. How the heroine meets and overcomes several moral dangers forms the substance of the narrative. Out of print, but available in libraries.

Similar works for boys and young men are less abundant, unfortunately, but the following should be mentioned:

51. Cross, John, *Let's Take the Hard Road.* The Cross Company, Box 389, Kenosha, WI, 1960 edition (B $3.95). This book for the adolescent boy urges purity in connection with the building of physical strength, capitalizing on the youth's interest in his body build. May perhaps lay too much emphasis on this aspect. Yet the focus of the book is on discipline and self-control.

Index

THE AUTHOR

Fr. Sattler, a Redemptorist ordained in 1943, has specialized in the theology of love, sexuality, marriage, family, bioethics and fundamental morality. He currently teaches in an emeritus position at the University of Scranton, where he was Professor of Theology from 1967-1988, with a brief hiatus to launch the (now discontinued) Castello Institute. This was a research arm of American Life League dedicated to all disciplines affecting the human person. From 1950-1957 he instructed many thousands of married and engaged couples in Pre-Cana Conference groups, through lectures and on television. He was also very active with the Christian Family Movement, and from 1957-1964 was Assistant Director of the Family Life Bureau of the National Catholic Welfare Conference (now the U.S. Catholic Conference). In this capacity he traveled widely in the U.S., Europe and Japan, also contributing many articles to various publications. In 1960 he received the Benemerenti Medal from Pope John XXIII for his work with married and engaged couples and the sex education of children and adolescents. In 1986 Fr. Sattler was a consultor to the Pontifical Institute for the Family in Rome. Fr. Sattler has directed retreats and Marriage Encounters. *Parents, Children and the Facts of Life* was considered a pioneering work when first published in 1953. Among Fr. Sattler's many other published works are *Together in Christ, Two to Get Ready, Sex Education in the Catholic Family, Sex Is Alive and Well and Flourishing Among Christians, Secular Humanism?, All About Love,* and *Challenging Children to Chastity.*